Dear Therese & Bob,
I hope you can relate to my story of mental health struggles and journey of recovery.

Tony W.

RESURGENT

(A MEMOIR OF HOPE AND HEALING)

by Tony Wentersdorf

Resurgent
A Memoir of Hope and Healing
by Tony Wentersdorf

©2021
All rights reserved. This book or any portion thereof
may not be reproduced or used in any manner whatsoever
without the express written permission of the publisher
except for the use of brief quotations in a book review.

Cover photo by Christie Kim on Unsplash
Back cover photo by Simon Wilkes on Unsplash

Printed in the United States of America
First Printing, May 2021

ISBN 978-163877006-0

Tony Wentersdorf
1350 Nicollet Mall, Apartment 607
Minneapolis, MN 55403
afwentersdorf@hotmail.com

This memoir is dedicated to all the therapists, mental health providers, and programs that have helped me over the past fifty years, especially the National Alliance on Mental Illness.

Musical Comedy Editions ◆ Minneapolis ◆ Portland OR

PREFACE

This memoir tells the story of my struggles with and continuing recovery from severe depression and anxiety. Part I relates my two-and-a-half years in a treatment center for the mentally ill, which I called Turnaround, where I lived from 1979 to 1981, and which had a profound and lasting impact on my life. Part II describes my week in a Minneapolis hospital psych ward in February 1995 which also impacted my life in a major way. Part III relates several experiences in which music played a major role in shaping my creative journey and helping me with my healing.

I have changed the name of the treatment center I lived at, as well as most of the names of the people I encountered along the way in deference to their rights to privacy.

TABLE OF CONTENTS

Introduction: Fives and Sevens		6
Part One: Turnaround		9
I	Starting a new Chapter	10
II	Learning the Ropes	14
III	Opening a Crack	16
IV	The Big Move	21
V	Uncovering the Core	23
VI	Creative Surge	29
VII	Back to Work	32
VIII	A Time to Celebrate	38
Part Two: Seven Days In-Patient		40
I	"I Can't go on any longer!"	41
II	Night-time Trauma	45
III	Hope on the Horizon	47
IV	A Reluctant Good-Bye	52
Part Three: My Life with Music		56
I	A Notable Journey	57
II	Nessun Dorma	61
III	The Open Stage from Hell	65
IV	From Love to Addiction	67
V	Winfield, Here I Come!	72
VI	Tangled Up in Dylan	79
Afterword		86

INTRODUCTION

Fives and Sevens

In examining the course of my life, I've noticed that the years ending in five have often been difficult, whereas those ending in seven have been more favorable. This begins with my birth on August 7, 1945 which was less than propitious since my birth mother abandoned me when I was just a few days old, and placed me in an orphanage. 1945 also marks the year the atom bomb was dropped on Hiroshima. The date 1947 was much more favorable since it marks the time I was adopted by a loving couple, Anna and Karl Wentersdorf.

This seemingly random confluence of dates continues throughout my life. In 1955, one year after emigrating to the U.S. from Germany, my dad, reluctantly placed me in a foster home because his very survival made it impossible for him to care for me. I remember being very unhappy there. But by 1957, things had improved considerably for my dad and me. In that year I was able to move back in with him in his Volkert Place apartment in Cincinnati. It was the year my love of classical music was born. It was also the year my dad's best friend, Arnold, moved in with us. Because of his love of opera, I was exposed to the operas of Verdi, Wagner, and Puccini, as well as famous tenors like McCormick and Caruso. In that year, I started writing my first poems.

In 1965, while a sophomore at Xavier University, I suffered a severe bout of depression which caused me to contemplate suicide. That year I published my first poem in the Xavier literary quarterly, *The Athenaeum*, called *Gas Jet Epitaph* in which a man kills himself by turning on the gas. However, by 1967, my situation had improved considerably. I was living in a dorm called Marion Hall with three other honors students. It was there that I met my first close friend Gene who introduced me to magic, and who influenced me in many ways. He and I shared lots of extracurricular activities such as jogging, eating pizzas, watching classic horror movies, listening to rock-n-roll music, and editing *The Athenaeum*.

1975 marked the low point in my adult life. That summer, after visiting my friends in Germany, I moved into a Minneapolis rooming house where I lived alone during that summer. The friends I had made in a University of Minnesota international residence called Namche House had all moved away, and I was left to fend for myself. I had no friends, no job, and no prospects for the future. Things got to the point I considered jumping off the Washington Avenue Bridge into the Mississippi, but by 1977 things had turned around completely. I now had a full-time job as a mail clerk at The Hennepin County Medical Center. I was living in a South Minneapolis rooming house where I made another good friend named Bob. I was also starting to date a woman named Edna.

1985 proved to be another difficult year. At the time I was attending a dysfunctional day-treatment program in West St. Paul where the therapists used abusive, shaming techniques like heavy-duty confrontations, yelling, physical restraints, and corner contracts (whereby clients were forced to stand in a corner for not conforming to therapists' demands). However, by 1987, I had left that program to attend a more positive day-treatment program where I got to know a very sympathetic therapist who helped me heal from my previous traumatic experiences. It was also the year that the Minnesota Twins won their first World Series. As a big baseball fan, I was caught up in the excitement of that October.

1995 marked another year in which my depression became so bad, I again thought of committing suicide. Instead, I admitted myself to a Minneapolis hospital mental health unit where I stayed for a week. By 1997, my situation had improved a lot once more. I fell in love with a woman named Cindy with whom I enjoyed a brief relationship. But by 1998 it was all over.

Even though 2005 was a fairly good year for me, some of my friends experienced various personal crises. The minister of my church committed suicide that summer. My best friend's wife came down with a severe case of Stills disease. And my primary therapist had a stroke from which he nearly died. But 2007 was a banner year for me. In May, I visited Germany for the first time in fifteen years. In June I completed a new CD of original songs called *Yin of my Yang*. In August, a play I had written about my experiences in the dysfunctional day-treatment program – *Cathect Adult* – was performed at the Minnesota Fringe Festival. And that summer I also fell in love again.

In 2015, I experienced another major bout of depression which caused me to go into a short-term crisis home, as well as attend a senior outpatient program in a Minneapolis hospital. But by 2017 things had improved once again. I was attending a very helpful Dialectical Behavior Therapy (DBT) program in St. Paul in which I learned new, valuable coping skills.

Although I don't know yet what 2025 will bring, I hope it won't continue the unfortunate 5/7 pattern. Right now I'm doing well and am very hopeful for the future.

PART ONE

TURNAROUND

PART ONE

TURNAROUND

I

I'm returning home from work one night to go to an abandoned farmhouse when my way is blocked by two snarling dogs that belong to my neighbor. To my relief, the neighbor boy restrains the dogs. Then suddenly, I find myself in a desolate lunar landscape. I run to get away from it when I see a train barreling in my direction. From the train I see a deadly cloud of fallout headed my way. I know for certain that if any of the poisonous gas reaches me, I will die instantly. So, I try to run away from the train as fast as I can. I reach some kind of elevator that can take me down to another level safe from the poisonous gas. Then I see an old college friend who is also running for his life. His hair has turned white, and his face is distorted with terror and approaching death. I hear an eerie song that goes: "When the rains came, they changed." This refrain is repeated many times. Finally, I reach what I thought was an elevator, but it turns out to be a large gym locker. I climb inside, lock myself in, and push the down button to escape the poison gas. But the down button won't work. So, I climb into another locker and lock myself inside again as the gas draws nearer. In the meantime, I keep hearing that refrain: "When the rains came, they changed." But this locker elevator won't move down either. Realizing that I'm about to die from inhaling the gas, I scream as loud as I can before my impending death. Then I wake up.

In the summer of 1979, my life turned around in a major way. It had already been an eventful year. In October 1978, I embarked on a new job as activities assistant in a nursing home where I was able to use my music for the first time as part of my work. In the spring of the next year, I attended an exciting, week-long camp for adults called Rec Lab. There I got to know a woman who used the autoharp to lead sing-a-longs. And in May of that year, I volunteered for a folk music festival that took place in the Cedar-Riverside area of Minneapolis. It was there that I met Stevie Beck, a woman who hosted an autoharp workshop, and would have a profound impact on my life.

Around this time, I was sharing a two-bedroom apartment with a friend of mine named Frank whom I had met three years before at a rooming house in South Minneapolis. He had become my closest friend in whom I was able to confide everything that was happening in my life. At the time, I was attending a weekly therapy group facilitated by a social worker in the new Government Center in downtown Minneapolis, as well as a men's group that Frank had invited me to join.

But despite these positive circumstances, I was not a happy camper. I was beset by frequent episodes of major depression and anxiety, especially while working in the nursing home, despite all the attempts of my supervisor to get me to stay. But in my heart, I knew that I didn't really want to work there any longer. Nor was the Government Center therapy group as helpful as it had been when I joined it three years earlier. I felt it was only addressing more superficial concerns and problems, instead of delving into the root causes of what was troubling me.

Fortunately, one member of the group told me about a new residential treatment center that had recently opened up in St. Paul which housed about twenty mentally ill adults. He added that this program used a variety of new, unconventional, experimental kinds of therapy like Yoga and bioenergetics. This was a radical departure from the cognitive-behavioral therapies employed by most hospital programs of the time. His description coincided with my long-time desire to find a kind of therapy that would address my underlying issues. These included my early abandonment by my birth mom, the eighteen months I spent in an orphanage, my emigration to the U.S., and my many subsequent moves. There were also other debilitating traumas that hadn't been addressed previously such as my anger towards my dad, my shame over my German heritage, and the guilt I felt about my sexuality fostered by my Catholic upbringing. I was also frustrated at the series of my low-level, mind-numbing, unsatisfying jobs that I had held since graduating from college. Indeed, my life was plagued by a glaring lack of self-esteem and self-confidence.

In the spring of 1979, I took the big plunge that would change my life forever. I quit my nursing home job to move into Harriet House, the residential treatment program I had heard about. But first I had to go through an intensive interview process to determine if I qualified to enter the program. This involved convincing the staff and some residents that I was sick enough to need this program. I told them of my traumatic background as well as all the counseling I had participated in over the past ten years. I assured them that I would work hard in therapy to better my situation. When I was accepted into the program, I breathed a huge sigh of relief. I was told that I could move there in July of that year. After my interview, I was given a brief tour of the facilities which consisted of two houses joined by a kind of skyway. The house I was assigned to live in had a large living room, a dining room, and kitchen. Upstairs were several bedrooms for the residents.

However, even after I'd been accepted in Harriet House, there were still several hurdles to jump over. For one thing, I had to give up the apartment I shared with my friend Frank. I also had to go on welfare since I didn't have enough money to pay the program costs. Going on welfare, or General Assistance as it was called, besides being very demeaning, also plunged me into poverty. Since I couldn't keep any of the money I had saved, I would have to live on about $10 dollars a month after all the program costs were taken care of. So, before moving into Harriett House, I sent my savings to my dad for safekeeping. That way I had something to draw from once I left the program.

After being accepted into Harriett House, my mood shifted immediately. I was exhilarated at the prospect of turning my life around. I couldn't wait to finally dig into some of my core issues that had kept me stuck for so long. Of course, the prospect of spending the next year or so in a residence of severely mentally ill adults was also very scary. A big part of me still believed that I was not sick enough to need this place. I also feared being around people who acted crazy like a dorm-mate I had while living in Marburg, Germany.

I spent that spring and summer before moving into Harriett House settling my affairs, planning my move, and sending my savings to my dad. I eagerly awaited my new life and wondered what the future held in store for me. For a few weeks, I floated on an incredible high that I had never experienced before. I spent many hours walking through a nearby college campus while reflecting on all the changes I was experiencing. I knew that I would miss my friend Frank, but I didn't miss not having to work any- more, at least while I was in the program. I also began having a lot of creative ideas for poems and songs. Around this time, I started taking autoharp lessons. And I attended some Open Mic nights at a coffeehouse on the West bank, as well as volunteered to play music at the nursing home where I used to work.

II

I'm a funny little guy without a cent or clue,
Sometimes I'm so lonesome, I get blue,
Sometimes I want someone to tie my shoe.

I love to sing, watch people dance,
I love to play and make romance,
I love to risk and take a chance.

When the sun comes up I feel alive,
And buzz like bees around a hive,
I'll always hope and always strive.

I eat with a spoon, see in the dark,
Leave my room to walk the park,
Light a match to catch a spark.

When the big day finally came, Frank helped me move the few things I could keep into the limited storage space the house had to offer. Some of my other things like furniture, I let him keep or give away. The approximately twenty Harriett House residents were all young adults from eighteen to thirty-five. At thirty-four, I was one of the oldest. They had a great variety of diagnoses, including depression, bi-polar disorder (then called manic depression), anxiety disorder, schizophrenia, schizo-affective disorder, obsessive compulsion, bulimia, and anorexia. I was given a small upstairs room in one of the two houses. It had a scenic view of the front yard.

During a brief orientation, I learned the house rules and customs. One main rule was: "No sexual contact between any house members." Anyone found having sex with another resident faced termination from the program. All residents were assigned daily chores such as cleaning bathrooms, vacuuming living and dining room floors, and mopping the kitchen floor. These chores, usually done first thing in the morning, were called "Genesis Cleaning." This was an apt name since the program director had formerly been a minister. In addition to cleaning chores, all residents were assigned to a two-person cooking crew. They prepared weekday dinners. For breakfast, lunch, and all weekend meals, residents were on their own. A young staff person named Randy was in charge of buying food which was stored in various kitchen cabinets, as well as two large refrigerators. Randy was a stickler for wholesome, non-junk food. He usually shopped for food at one of the neighboring coops which were just then becoming popular. I remember eating a lot of granola for breakfast.

In addition to Randy, Harriett House had a full-time director named Kurt, two full-time therapists, a Yoga teacher, a bioenergetics instructor, and a maintenance man. During an orientation session, I found out that the residents stayed in the program from an average of one to two years. The program itself was divided into four parts called Phase I, II, III, and IV. Phase I was designed for new residents, at the end of which, if they successfully graduated, they formally joined the program and began the serious work of full-time therapy. To pass into Phase II, residents were required to learn certain therapy terms. One was called kicking and pounding, whereby residents lay on their backs while kicking their legs and pounding their arms onto a mat. Another was an anger reduction technique called racketing in which residents beat down on a pillow with a tennis racket while yelling out their rage.

Phase II comprised the meat of the program during which residents worked full-time on their therapy goals. In Phase III they either attended school or worked part-time. And Phase IV came after residents graduated from the program to move out on their own again. However, they were encouraged to maintain their connection with Turnaround by attending a weekly evening therapy group. They could also keep their primary therapist for a year after graduating.

Besides each morning's Genesis Cleaning, there weekly groups such as a therapy group, Yoga, bioenergetics, and house meetings. These, I soon found out, often got very intense, especially when a resident got confronted for breaking a house rule, acting inappropriately, injuring themselves or others, acting crazy, or threatening suicide.

All residents were assigned a primary therapist whom they saw once a week and with whom they worked on personal, interpersonal, and vocational goals. Everyone was required to attend Yoga and therapy group. The more seasoned residents often added the bioenergetics group although it was not mandatory. This was one of the most unconventional groups I'd ever witnessed. Instead of just talking about issues, residents were encouraged to discharge feelings like rage, fear, and sadness. The emphasis was on doing body work as a way of getting in touch with powerful emotions.

My favorite group quickly became the weekly 10 o'clock Yoga group led by a tall, handsome African American man named Brian who guided us in a series of Yoga postures that ended with a mindfulness meditation. This group had an enormous healing effect on me. As a matter of fact, I still practice Yoga and mindfulness meditation to this day.

In addition to participating in the various groups and individual therapy, I was also assigned a big sister named Mary. She became my mentor by walking me through the various house customs and traditions. I liked her right away because she was easy to talk with and very supportive. Since we both loved cooking, I asked her to become my cooking partner.

Moving into Harriett House was my first experience in communal living since I lived in two college dorms as an undergraduate and graduate student. But this would be a totally different experience since all the residents were mentally ill.

III

Grow, little seed, grow,
Grow, little seed, grow,
Don't mind the weather,
Don't mind the snow,
Just grow, little seed, grow.

Once I had a little seed,
I put it in the ground,
Covered it with frost and snow,
Now it can't be found,
Now it can't be found.

Once there was a little boy,
They told him what to say,
He wouldn't listen to their words,
Now he's gone away,
Now he's gone away.

After moving into Harriett House, I was assigned an individual therapist in his early sixties named Arthur. I liked him right away because he was kind-hearted, a good listener, and very insightful. After I told him about my traumatic childhood, he responded sympathetically. He not only understood the enormous rage I felt towards my dad, but also encouraged me to express myself creatively. I'll never forget what he said after I showed him some of my recent poetry: "Tony, are all your poems this angry?"

I never realized that I was angry at all, so out of touch was I with my feelings. However, Arthur didn't say this to make me feel bad. On the contrary, he picked up right away that I stuffed my feelings. In the past, any setbacks quickly turned into long debilitating bouts of depression.

It also helped that Arthur was a writer. He explained to me that he too had a hard time finding his way. In fact, he had tried for years to conform to everyone else's expectations by becoming a minister because he felt it was his duty to help others. But that wasn't where his heart was at. What he really wanted to do was to write. So, finally he started doing just that when he was in his mid-thirties. Once he told me, "Tony, if a creative person stifles his creativity, it almost invariably leads to mental illness of some kind. In your case, it's depression."

One time Arthur told me an unforgettable story to illustrate what happens to someone who tries to conform to others' expectations at the cost of his own dreams. He read about a scientific experiment in which some fleas were put inside a glass jar. The jar was sealed tight with a lid. Then the fleas were left inside the jar for an extended time. However, when the lid was finally opened, the unexpected happened. Instead of the fleas flying out of the jar, they stayed on the bottom.

Arthur quickly picked up from my mannerisms that I was extremely nervous. I was wound up as tight as a spring, and tried hard to always say the right thing. He encouraged me to join the bioenergetics group as soon as possible, so that I could learn to identify and discharge the feelings I held locked inside my body. He was convinced that by letting out my repressed rage, I could deal with my chronic, recurring bouts of depression.

I told Arthur how angry I was at my dad for not encouraging me to be creative, especially as far as my writing was concerned. I told him that, once when I showed my dad a story I had written, he ended up criticizing it by marking down all the mistakes. Arthur also thought that my addiction to folk music was a way of getting back at my dad because I knew that I could never make a living playing music. I told Arthur about my succession of dead-end, mind-numbing jobs which didn't allow for creative expression.

It wasn't long before I witnessed my first anger work. It was in a therapy group where a young woman named Emma expressed her anger at her mom for favoring her younger sister. Emma stood up to pound a couple of large pillows with a tennis racket while screaming out her rage. "I hate you, mom! Why did you favor my baby sister? You weren't there for me when I needed you! You don't love me! I hate you! Fuck you!"

I was shocked because I hadn't heard people use cuss words like that since I had worked in a factory ten years before. But, as I was soon to discover, this was a core part of the program. After Emma had discharged her anger, she collapsed into a chair and stated sobbing. Then one of the therapists held her. This was certainly the most intense therapy work I had ever witnessed, a far cry from anything in my previous groups.

With Arthur's gentle coaching, I also decided on my first personal, interpersonal, and vocational goals. These included talking with others on a feeling level, doing intense body work to discharge my rage, and pursuing my creative interests like playing the autoharp, composing songs, and writing poems and stories. I found out that talking on a feeling level with others was the most difficult goal to achieve. I wasn't used to talking about myself to people I didn't know, much less doing it on a feeling level.

As the summer progressed, I gradually grew more comfortable with the other Harriett House residents. I felt as if I was going through a kind of honeymoon. I got up each morning eager to begin a new day of uncharted adventures. I grew close to my big sister Mary. I enjoyed cooking dinner with her. Some of the women residents began reaching out to me even though I was hesitant to approach them. However, I didn't feel as comfortable around the men. And most of them avoided me. For the most part, I enjoyed doing my house chores, even when it was cleaning toilets. And I quickly learned the Harriett House terminology. While I looked forward to structured groups like Yoga, therapy group, and even house meetings, I had a harder time socializing in unstructured settings. Hanging out with others was still anathema! By the end of the summer, I helped organize a variety show in which the residents roasted the program director Kurt. One woman played the piano, another the flute. One talented young man played a Steve Forbert song on his guitar. I sang my new song, *Grow, Little Seed, Grow*, while accompanying myself on the autoharp. Another guy read some of his poetry. People came up with all kinds of funny anecdotes about Kurt during the roast segment of the show. Since he had a good sense of humor, he took it all in stride. Not only did the evening turn out to be a tremendous success, but it also made me feel more like I belonged.

IV

I feel like I've been here before,
I don't know why, don't know what for,
Sometimes there's a lot of pain,
Sometimes there is too much change.
Don't always know what I'm going through,
Often don't know what to do.
I try so hard to find my way,
Look for one to share my day,
Sometimes I feel very sad,
Sometimes like I'm going mad.
Don't always want to trip and fall,
I wanna make some sense of it all.

Just as I started feeling comfortable in Harriett House, a huge change loomed on the horizon. In the fall, the program was replaced by another more conventional model. The current therapy staff was replaced by new providers. The residents were given the option of either staying at Harriett House with the new staff, or moving to Minneapolis to a new facility where they could keep the same therapists they'd come to depend on. This new program was called Turnaround. It was housed in a former board-and-care home located in a large stately mansion overlooking a freeway near a scenic city park.

I decided to move into Turnaround with about a dozen other Harriett House residents as well as the same number of new ones. Besides moving my own things into the new place, I also stayed busy helping the higher functioning residents unpack boxes, load our van, and sort through all the stuff to be moved. Because the board-and-care had been so neglected, we spent the next few weeks vacuuming carpets, cleaning bathrooms, sweeping and mopping floors, washing windows, and doing many other tasks. Even when everyone had moved into the new place, there was still a lot of work to be done to make the place more inviting.

During several house meetings, the staff organized volunteers to repaint the living room, dining room, kitchen, staff offices, and resident bedrooms. They also bought new sofas, armchairs, lamps, and desks. I joined several others to paint the upstairs bedrooms. This project took several weeks during which new residents were able to bond with the old ones. Painting gave me even more a sense of belonging. At one point one of my fellow painters commented, "Welcome to Turnaround, Tony."

During this time, I was assigned to share a large bedroom on the third floor with a man named Ernie. It was the same man who had read his rather crude poetry at the summer roast. At Harriett House I had avoided him because I was afraid of his devil-may-care, rebellious attitude. In fact, he was often confronted by staff people during house meetings for his foul language and angry outbursts. But to my relief we hit it off almost immediately. We both shared a mutual interest in poetry and Bob Dylan songs. Like me, he played guitar and harmonica. Ernie turned out to be a great roommate. With one major exception, we seldom had any conflicts.

Around this time, I decided to switch to a woman therapist named Lisa, not because I didn't appreciate Arthur's support, but because I felt more comfortable working on my abandonment issues with a woman. I also thought she could help me deal with my grief at the loss of my adoptive mom. Lisa, along with Kurt, had started the Harriett House program several years before. Fortunately, Arthur didn't take my asking for a new therapist personally. I continued to see him occasionally, especially when Lisa was on vacation. She and I hit it off immediately. I really liked her nurturing yet firm approach.

V

I'm singing hymns in church with my father. I tell him about a German hymn written by Martin Luther called "O Haupt voll Blut und Wunden" (O Sacred Head A-bleeding) that I loved as a boy. My dad explains to me why this hymn is so significant for me because it refers to Christ's suffering on the cross. He adds that I too suffered a lot after the death of my adoptive mom when I was five. I suddenly feel the urge to cry out loud, something I've never done before. Then I feel my dad's comforting hand caress my face.

Just before moving to Minneapolis, I successfully phased out of Phase I to become full-fledged member of Turnaround. With Lisa as my new therapist, I peeled away more and more layers of my resistance. I dug even deeper into my core issues of abandonment, loss of my adopting mom, anger at my dad, frustration over my thankless jobs, shame about being German, Catholic guilt, and the loneliness of not fitting in. I told her how I hated moving all the time as a boy, having to start a new school every couple of years, being bullied by the other kids in junior high, being made to feel ashamed of my emerging sexuality, and having to look for work.

I now embarked on the work I needed to do to access all the pent-up emotions in my body such as rage, sadness, and fear. Soon I did my first serious piece of body work. Arthur, who was facilitating group at the time, asked me to tell people how I saw myself. I said, "I feel lonely, cut-off from others, and alienated, like a square peg in a round hole; stiff, formal, and definitely not cool like my roommate Ernie." With Arthur's encouragement, I lay on my back on a mat. I kicked and pounded my arms and legs as hard as I could while screaming out my rage. My body began to shake and tremble. Then I started laughing hysterically. Arthur encouraged me to keep breathing while asking me to repeat, "Poor Tony, poor Tony." When I had finished my work on the mat, he held me while saying in a gentle voice, "Tony, welcome to Turnaround." For me this was a very cathartic moment!

Another time, after I had had a nightmare about my dad in which he attacked me with a butcher knife, Kurt, who was leading group at the time, asked me to do some anger work. While he played the role of my dad, Kurt urged me to push against him as hard as I could while yelling, "I hate you! I hate you!" Afterwards, I felt a wild mix of emotions, everything from rage to fear to grief. My whole body ached from the torrent of feelings I had just released. I felt raw and vulnerable.

Another time, Lisa asked me to describe what my rage looked like. Because I was born on August 7, 1945, one day after the first atom bomb exploded over Hiroshima, I immediately imagined my rage to be as powerful as that bomb. I became the bomb while screaming out and pounding on a pillow with my clenched fists until I was spent. When I had finished, Lisa held me. My anger subsided quickly and turned into sobs. Afterwards, I was filled with a profound sense of peace, or like a baby who has just taken his first steps. I realized that I was finally penetrating the core of my deepest feelings.

It was during this time that I also experienced my first major conflict. It happened with a woman named Edna who had befriended me earlier while I was still at Harriett House. I don't recall what started the conflict. It may have been something I said to her that made her angry. She in turn yelled at me. I completely lost control, yelled back at her at the top of my lungs, and pushed her away violently. After that she went ballistic. One of the residents who witnessed the scene told me I needed to set up a fair fight with her.

A fair fight was a technique developed by the program to resolve disputes. The two conflicting parties had to meet with each other while a third neutral person served as a go-between to make sure things didn't get out of hand. The two antagonists then took turns spelling out their grievances while using only I-statements. I was confronted at the next house meeting for behaving violently. I had to pick someone to moderate my fair fight with Edna. At first, I didn't know who to ask, but I finally picked my big sister Mary because I felt most comfortable with her. She in turn was willing to help me.

When the big day finally came, Edna and I met in one of the empty offices while Mary moderated the fair fight to make sure things didn't get out of control. Edna told me how angry she was when I pushed her. She added that she was scared of my rage. I in turn expressed what had made me angry, while also apologizing for pushing her. We were both careful to use only I statements. In this way we were able to resolve our conflict and work things out between us. Although we came to an uneasy truce, we never felt as comfortable around each other afterwards.

Besides fair fights, another valuable technique I learned at Turnaround was organizing support groups for myself when I was feeling down and there were no therapists to call on. This often occurred on weekends when the staff was gone. Soon other residents also asked me to be in their support groups. This had the added benefit of helping me get closer to people.

During that first fall at Turnaround, not all was therapy and hard work. We had a fun Halloween party at which people dressed up in all kinds of imaginative costumes. I remember one guy dressed as Count Dracula. And on the week before Christmas, we had a big party for which I helped organize the music. Some of the people who had participated in the summer roast at Harriett House performed again. We all sang Christmas carols led by Kurt and Lisa, while one of the newer residents played the piano. I again brought out my autoharp. It was a great way to end the year and the decade.

During Christmas vacation, I visited my dad in Cincinnati where I had grown up and where he was teaching college English. I asked him to come to Minneapolis to join me in a family therapy session with Arthur. But things didn't turn out as I had hoped. When I told my dad that I had talked to Arthur about him (my dad) being gay, he got very angry with me. He asked me what else I told Arthur about him. He emphasized that what he told me was meant in strict confidence, that he didn't expect me to blab it to some therapist. He added that he was no longer comfortable in confiding in me. And he certainly wasn't about to travel all the way to Minneapolis to be made into the bad guy in a family therapy session. When I returned to Turnaround, I felt very shaken about the rift between us. Despite my increased involvement with people at Turnarouund, I still found it hard to make new friends. I also remained very awkward in unstructured settings. I recall one resident named Crystal telling me once that she saw me as always being busy doing things, but not getting close to people. That really hit home because it triggered my feelings of loneliness when I was growing up. I also didn't know what to do when someone was having a psychotic episode. Another problem was that some of the more aggressive men got into the habit of talking my ear off. Because I felt it was my duty to listen, I found it hard to break off these one-way dialogues.

Since smoking was permitted on the premises, a lot of the men as well as some of the women spent a lot of their free time smoking in the living room where they liked to hang out between therapy groups. Because I had such a hard time socializing, I made myself two new interpersonal goals: hanging out with others in unstructured groups, and talking about myself. Both of these goals were extremely difficult because I often didn't know what to say. I was so used to listening to others, or asking them questions, but I was afraid to initiate conversations. Yet, I was determined to change some of my old, ingrained behaviors so I could climb out of my shell. Thus, I started spending about half an hour twice a week just hanging out in the living room while others were chatting and smoking.

The intense therapy I was now experiencing in Phase II of the program soon took a physical toll on me. After returning from my Christmas vacation, I got sick with double pneumonia. Even though I wasn't hospitalized, I spent a lot of time in bed and missed a lot of what was going on in the house.

As soon as I got better, I continued my intense therapy work with Lisa. I remember one time she had me place my birth mother on a pillow. Then she asked me to beat on the pillow as hard as I could while yelling, "Why did you abandon me? Why did you leave me? I hate you! I hate you!" Lisa encouraged me to let it all out. Afterwards, my body felt as limp as a dish rag that had just been wrung out. Lisa then held me while I cried softly in her arms. In that moment she felt like a new mom.

During the winter, Monday evening house meetings became more and more heated as other residents also began uncovering their core issues. Fortunately, I was seldom confronted by the staff or other residents except for that fair fight with Edna. I always did my chores and showed up for groups on time.

There was one unforgettable house meeting, however, when things got really tense between me and Ernie. He was frequently brought up for inappropriate behavior, uncontrollable rage, and foul language. Usually we got on fine, but there was one time when things between us came to a head. Even though sexual contact between house residents was forbidden, Ernie fell in love with a woman named Amy. They started sleeping together in Ernie's bed which was next to mine. They made love while I was trying to go to sleep. Even though I got upset, I was too frightened to say anything about it because I was scared that Ernie would get angry with me if I called him on it. So I let things slide for several weeks. But finally, I just couldn't stand it anymore. Something inside me told me I needed to speak up to maintain my self-respect, even at the risk of a major confrontation with Ernie and Amy.

Then, one memorable Monday evening that winter, I screwed up my courage to confront them on their behavior at the house meeting. But instead of the angry outburst from Ernie that I was expecting, I got overwhelming support from the other residents who assured me I had done the right thing. Nor did Ernie and Amy get mad at me. At least they didn't show it. I now think that Ernie secretly respected me for standing up to him. After that, they stopped having sex in our room. I was surprised that neither of them was suspended from the program, but I think it was because they contributed so much to Turnaround in other ways.

There was another time when I was able to assert myself in a difficult situation. On the third-floor landing outside my bedroom was a TV set that people often watched at night. There was a house rule that people were supposed to be in bed by eleven p.m. so they wouldn't disturb the others who were trying to sleep. But as time went on, several guys on the floor ignored the rule by keeping the TV on loud until midnight or even later. Since I had a hard time getting to sleep, I often stayed up tossing and turning while the TV blared. After several weeks of this, I finally had enough. One night when the noise was especially loud, I burst out of my room in my underwear to shout, "Turn off that damned TV!" The guys were so startled by my unaccustomed outburst, that they quickly slunk away. They had never seen me get this mad before. After that, things quieted down for a while. But then it happened again. Finally, I got so fed up, I brought it up at the next house meeting. Once more I got a lot of support from the other residents, and the behavior stopped. I think I also gained some respect from the guys involved.

With the coming of spring, I started to feel emotions other than rage and anger, such as sadness and fear. As I felt myself softening, I was able to access my long-repressed grief at losing my adopting mom. With Lisa's gentle coaxing, I also started letting go of a lot of the shame and guilt I had acquired as a teenager because of my sexual feelings.

VI

Free your musical spirit,
Free your musical soul.
Sing it out loud from to the rafters,
Sing it out loud and bold.

There's times when I feel like crying,
There's times when I'm sad and blue,
There's always something a-dying,
But there's always something new.

Music brings joy to the lonely,
Puts a smile on the saddest face,
There's a song inside every person,
And each song has its time and place.

So, don't go hide in your cellars,
Don't bury your face in the ground,
Stand up and look at the sunshine,
And let the music resound!

One of the benefits of doing all the hard work in therapy was that I was loosening up considerably. My determined efforts to hang out and reveal things about myself resulted in my getting closer to others, and in making friends along the way. The other benefit was an enormous surge in creative energy. I spent many hours in my room playing the autoharp. I even got a neat compliment from my teacher Stevie. After one lesson, she told me that of all her students, I had made the most progress in the shortest period of time. She thought I'd soon be ready to branch out on my own. During this time, I got lots of ideas for new songs which I copied down in my journal. I also continued attending Open Mic nights at the Coffeehouse Extempore.

In the spring, I attended a workshop on performance and stage presence. I'll never forget the instructor's comment when I first performed a song of mine. He said, "You look like a man who has just been hanged." That sure shook me up. However, as time went on, I gradually made progress. As I got more experience singing my songs, my confidence grew. During this time, I also organized a group of musicians to play at the nursing home I had worked at the year before. One was a man from my earlier men's group. Another was a young woman I used to work with. And the third was a Harriett House resident. We got together regularly to practice songs. Our nursing home performances were well received by my former supervisor and the residents.

I now began looking for a part-time volunteer job that took me outside the house. In June, I found a job I never would have dreamed of seeking before coming to Turnaround. For many years, I had spent hours listening to the radio, first to a KSTP talk radio station, and later to Minnesota Public Radio where Garrison Keillor was broadcasting his new *Prairie Home Companion* show. I often fantasized about playing on the show myself.

My dream of getting on the radio finally came true when I found a job volunteering at KFAI *Fresh Air Radio* that summer. KFAI was located on the third floor of Walker United Methodist Church in South Minneapolis. My job was to assist the producer of a show called *Live from the Extemp*, which began at midnight every Friday night and featured folk singers at the coffeehouse. Several times when the regular host couldn't make it, I was even able to DJ an hour-long show by playing my favorite records. It was a thrill to be on the air for the first time in my life. That summer, one of the employees asked me to write a story for the KFAI program guide. For my topic I chose Open Stage venues in the Twin Cities. I spent many hours working on this project. My article was published in the fall.

During this time, I was also able to secure a gig at a small coffeehouse in South Minneapolis called The Blue Heron Café where I was paid in tips. One week I earned eleven dollars. It seemed like a fortune, given the fact that I was only earning $10 a month on general assistance. I played at the Blue Heron several times that summer. One time I invited my friend Marshall, whom I'd gotten to know at a Christmas party held by my former nursing home supervisor. He joined me on his dobro and we soon became friends. Although he was a talented musician, he was on the shy side like me, but he loved to perform. He had a quirky sense of humor that always made me laugh. He did a great Elvis impersonation that I always got a kick out of. We spent a lot of time talking, taking walks round the city lakes, eating out, and playing music. We also played at the nursing home where he now worked as an activities assistant.

During the summer, I took another big step to boost my confidence, when I trained to become a resident counselor at Turnaround. In this new position I was able to support the other house residents during the weekends when the staff was not available. In case of a crisis, my job was to call the staff. Fortunately, there were no crises during my watch. But I learned to do a lot of active listening. I also helped residents set up support groups as needed. All in all, it proved to be a very rewarding summer filled with many new adventures.

VII

I've seen them by the hundreds filling out the forms,
I've seen them by the thousands trying to follow norms,
They're sitting in their little offices day after day
Behind their little typewriters, typing their lives away.
They've all got a fix on security
Until the day to retire
Comes too soon one bright morning,
Their hopes and dreams expire.

I've seen them by the hundreds sitting in their rooms,
I've seen them by the thousands buried in the gloom,
They're waiting for some fantasy to take away their pain,
They're popping pills and sedatives to ease their aching brains.
They've all got a fix on loneliness,
And wait for someone to come,
To take away their emptiness,
And give them back the sun.

Early in the fall, I began to feel some pressure from Lisa and the other therapists to move into Phase III of the program. Although I had been eager to move into Phase II, Phase III was another matter. I was definitely not looking forward to job hunting since that was one of the things I'd always been afraid of. It also meant that my moving out date was drawing nearer. I didn't want to be on my own again, separated from all that support. Despite my misgivings, however, I soon made it a new goal to look for a paying job. But this time I was determined to find work in which I could use my creative gifts of music and writing, yet one where I wouldn't get depressed as I had while working in the nursing home. Since I had already gained considerable confidence from my volunteer job at the radio station and my part-time paid job as resident counselor, I felt very upbeat.

I subsequently embarked on a series of informational interviews. The first of these was with an editor of the Minneapolis Star Tribune. I also contacted several music stores including Schmitt Music in downtown Minneapolis where I got a chance to speak with Mr. Schmitt himself. He turned out to be very friendly.

To my delight, I was hired at Schmitt Music in January 1981. But the work itself wasn't what I had envisioned. Instead of being hired to do something creative like helping sell musical instruments or teaching guitar or autoharp, my job consisted of typing up sheet music orders. Luckily, the work was only part-time, so I could continue to live at Turnaround to work on my therapy. But I found the work itself extremely boring. My back quickly got sore from all that sitting. It reminded me of my unhappy years at the large research library in Marburg, Germany where I worked in the early 1970s, and where I spent endless hours copying catalog cards. At Schmitt Music I had next to no contact with my fellow employees, most of whom I found hard to approach. Any contact that was made depended on me. Nor did I get on with my new supervisor who gave me a hard time because of my slow progress. The fastest I could type was only thirty words a minute which was nothing to write home about. When she also discovered that I lived in a halfway house, her attitude towards me became even more frosty. I quit before I could be fired.

Because of my frustration on the job, I did a lot of anger work with Lisa: kicking, pounding, racketing, and other discharging, so I could vent my rage at having to do this mind-numbing work. To my immense relief, I received a lot of support from the other residents after leaving Schmitt Music. I also had another enormous surge of creative energy during which I wrote a lot of new songs.

One of these, called *Blind Man*, was about a blind man who sold pencils on Nicollet Mall. When I played the song for a blind resident named Sarah, she immediately broke down in tears. I was as amazed as gratified. It made me realize for the first time that my songs could move others. Around this time, I experienced a new emotion - exuberant joy. I wrote a song that captures this feeling called *Born Long Ago*.

A few weeks after quitting Schmitt Music, I returned to the job hunt. But this time I was determined to find something more satisfying. And then in March 1981, I finally hit the jackpot! I found the job of my dreams! I was hired as a community education coordinator at an elementary school in South Minneapolis called Lyndale Elementary School. I could hardly believe my good fortune. Here I could finally use my creative skills and get paid for it! The work consisted of planning the community ed classes for spring. Since I only had to work twenty hours a week, I could still attend Turnaround groups. Not only did I begin my new job at Lyndale Community School in the beginning of March, but in April I taught my very first community ed class at another elementary school called Pratt. It was a class called Autoharp Basics. It was made up of four enthusiastic students, one of whom not only became a good friend, but also began using the autoharp in her work as a nursing home activities director. Besides our love of music, we also shared a common German heritage.

As excited as I was about my new job, I found some of the duties to be overwhelming. I was required to do things I had never done before like take charge of an entire community ed program, recruit instructors, set up spring classes, handle registrations, work with the janitor to make sure that classrooms were ready, and work with kids. The scariest part for me was supervising open gym for grade school kids. Since I had hardly ever worked with kids before, I was afraid that I wouldn't be able to control the kids if they acted up. I knew I wasn't cut out to be a disciplinarian. Fortunately, I was able to work on any issues that came up with Lisa and in therapy group. My favorite part of my new job was teaching autoharp which turned out to be a real labor of love.

And as if this new coordinator job wasn't daunting enough, I had to face an even greater challenge that summer when my community ed supervisor assigned me to work as an aide at another elementary school in Northeast Minneapolis. My job was to work with elementary age kids in a city-wide sports arts program, supervising games and activities. This was also something I had never done before. Fortunately, I shared the job with another aide who had more experience. Even though I often felt like running away, I decided to face the music. During one therapy group, a resident suggested that I get support for myself by asking someone in the program to accompany me to the school for the first few days. An attractive young woman named Karen, who had recently joined Turnaround, offered to go with me to the school during the first week. Not only did I feel an instant rapport with her, but it was good to have her along because she had lots of good ideas of things to do with the kids.

As the time for the sports arts program got closer, my anxiety grew until I had a hard time sleeping nights. Yes, this was certainly the scariest task I had ever faced, even scarier than working in a factory after dropping out of grad school, or teaching English in Germany. In order to boost my confidence and gather ideas, I borrowed a book from the library which contained lots of kids' activities and games.

When the big day to work at the school finally came, Karen accompanied me. I also met the other aide I was to work with. Both had lots of ideas for keeping the kids occupied. As for the kids, they turned out to be less rambunctious than I had feared. I surprised myself by actually enjoying games like pickle-in-the-middle, tug-of-war, and hide-and-seek, as long as I didn't have to be in charge, or deal with discipline problems. The other aide did most of that. I breathed a huge sigh every time my tour of duty was done at the end of the afternoon. Even though my fears never diminished, I managed to get through that summer unscathed. And I was immensely grateful to Karen for her support.

Whereas I found it stressful to work with the kids, I quickly learned to enjoy my responsibilities as a resident counselor. In fact,

I found the work satisfying and rewarding. I liked being able to support the newer residents. Fortunately, no one had a major crisis or psychotic episode while I was on duty. I spent most of my time helping people set up support groups, talking one-on-one, or just hanging out. Sometimes, when things got slow late at night, I was even able to sleep in a downstairs office. The only crises happened when I wasn't there to witness them. One time, for example, a new resident committed suicide. Another time a young woman was raped by an older native American man outside the house. But I didn't have to deal with these events. I only heard about them later.

After completing my summer sports arts school aide job, I was assigned to a serve as an aide at yet another community school in the fall. This time it was a high school in North Minneapolis. It was an ideal job for me because I really liked the community ed coordinator, a retired air force veteran named George for whom this community ed job was a second career. George was very easy to talk to and treated me like a son. He carefully explained my new job duties. They involved helping him plan winter community ed classes, interviewing prospective instructors, making coffee, and getting classrooms ready for evening classes. The other thing I liked about this job was that I no longer had to work with kids, just adults. I also found it much less stressful to work as an aide instead of being in charge as a coordinator.

Unfortunately, George had to quit late that fall because of a near-fatal heart attack. I really missed him. For the next two and a half years, I was assigned to another elementary school in South Minneapolis, Armatage Community School. There I also worked as an aide, this time with a woman coordinator who had been there for many years. I didn't get along with her as well as I had with George, but I benefited a lot from her on-the-job training. While working at these community schools, I continued teaching autoharp, to which I later added harmonica and journal writing.

There was one other big event that summer. Some of the men in my former men's group persuaded me to have surgery on my most tender organ since I had a condition called phimosis which made having sex with a woman quite painful. A doctor at

Hennepin County Medical Center persuaded me to have a partial circumcision to correct this problem. I had part of my foreskin removed. The surgery itself wasn't as painful as I feared, but the doctor first had to insert a hypodermic syringe straight into the tip of my penis to administer the anesthetic. And that hurt like hell! But after the surgery I soon recovered with no negative side effects.

Around this time the Turnaround staff hired some therapists from the University of Minnesota Human Sexuality Program to give workshops on sexuality and relationships. That got me thinking of dating again. I put in several personal ads in a couple of Minneapolis papers in hopes of finding a partner.

I also did some important work with Lisa on my sexual issues. I told her that most of my previous relationships with women were unsatisfying because of the conflicted feelings around my sexuality. As a boy and young man, I had next to no contact with girls or women since I attended an all-boys' Catholic high school and an all-men's Catholic college. I was very shy around girls growing up. It didn't help that I was taught that masturbation was a mortal sin, punishable by an eternity in hell. Consequently, I didn't start dating until I was a freshman in college. Even then I felt more comfortable with my male friends. Lisa encouraged me to accept myself as a sexual being, one time even suggesting that I see a masseuse for a sexual massage. She told me that she was trained as a masseuse. She certainly had a tender touch. But there was never anything sexual between us.

This was fortunate because about a year after I left Turnaround, there was a big scandal when it was discovered that Lisa got involved sexually with two of her clients. The word got out because one of the residents involved revealed it to the press. As a result, Kurt and Lisa were fired and the entire program was shut down by the county. I'm glad I was no longer around to witness all this because it would have been quite traumatic. As it was, when I found out that the Turnaround program was closed, it sent me spiraling down into a deep depression. In fact, things got so bad I quit my community ed job to enter yet another therapy program!

VIII

I wish I was born long ago,
I wish I was born long ago,
If I was born long ago, I'd make them green hills grow.

There's magic in the mountains and the sea,
There's magic in the mountains and the sea.
There's magic in the sea and my true love next to me.

This music's always on my mind,
This music's always on my mind,
This music's on my mind, and it won't leave me behind.

Is heaven very far away?
Is heaven very far away?
If heaven's far away, I'll go up there and stay.

Tell them when I'm dead and gone,
Tell them when I'm dead and gone,
Tell them when I'm gone to remember this one song.

As the summer wore on, and I'd been at Turnaround for almost two-and- --a-half years, I felt pressure from both Lisa and Kurt to graduate, which made me anxious because I was afraid of losing the support of the staff and residents. What made the situation a bit less scary was the prospect of moving into Phase IV. This meant that I could continue to see Lisa in individual therapy for a year after graduating. I could also keep attending the Tuesday evening outpatient therapy group to get support from other program graduates.

To prepare for my departure, I began to look for an apartment. I didn't have to look for long. I soon found an affordable one-bedroom apartment in South Minneapolis whose landlord lived next door and gave me a discount on the rent for mowing the lawn in the summer and shoveling snow in winter. That was fortunate since my new part-time community ed job didn't pay that well.

Towards the end of October, the big day finally came for me to graduate from the program. By this time most of the residents I'd known at Harriett House, as well as many at Turnaround, had already left. Graduating was a proud moment indeed! I received a small medallion, a graduation certificate, and the well wishes of the residents and staff. I got lots of hugs all around, and was praised for the hard work I had done during my time in the program. I looked forward to continuing my therapy with Lisa.

Yes, Turnaround marked a major milestone in my life. For one thing, I learned to feel things I'd never felt before. I learned to identify and discharge feelings like anger, fear, and sadness. I was able to experience joy. I got to know several good friends with whom I planned to stay in touch. I became less rigid and blocked. I became more self-assured in my jobs as resident counselor, radio DJ, community ed aide, coordinator, and teacher. I received a lot of support from therapists like Lisa, Arthur, and Kurt, as well as from house residents. I learned to stand up for myself, to take on new leadership roles, and to have more confidence in myself. Finally, I found a fulfilling job!

Best of all, my creativity flourished as never before as I wrote a lot of new songs, performed at various Open Mics, coffeehouses, and the nursing home where I used to work. I was happy teaching community ed classes. I formed a close bond with my new friend Marshall. Yes, my time at Turnaround marked a major turnaround in my life.

PART TWO

SEVEN DAYS IN-PATIENT

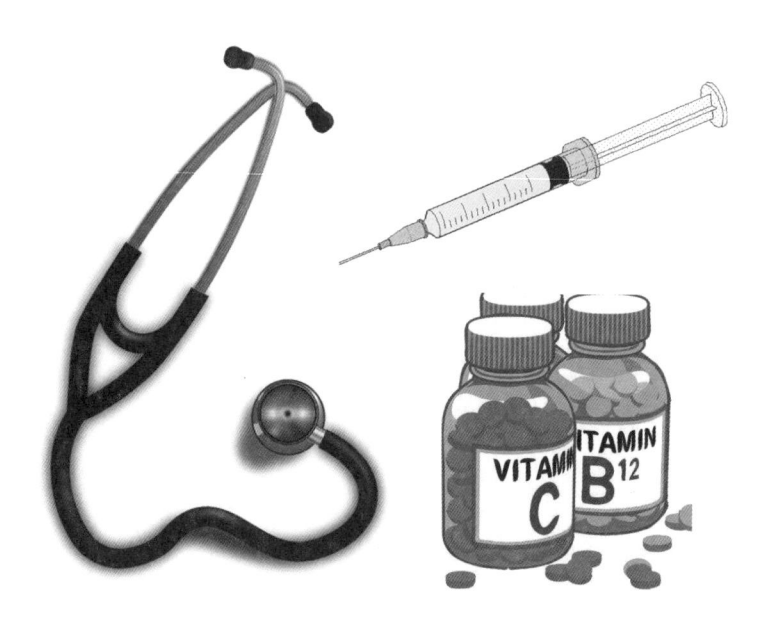

PART TWO

SEVEN DAYS IN-PATIENT

Seven days in-patient,
Perched on the edge of madness,
I struggle to maintain my sanity,
While the world outside goes crazy.
I pace the confines of my padded room,
While I try to tame the thoughts
That threaten to lay me waste.
I find peace inside the locked ward
Of my feelings.

I

"I just can't go on any longer! I can't keep living like this. I need help and I need it badly! Suicide is just a jump away, or all the pills I've got at home – five bottles worth."

These thoughts spun around in my head while I waited in E.R. to be admitted to the psych unit of the hospital, and heard a young woman screaming. They had just put her in seclusion where she kept crying out that her rights were being violated. She demanded to see her doctor so she could tell him how unfairly they were treating her.

"All I wanted was some stitches," she kept shouting. But the nurses who were frantically trying to deal with her, told her she couldn't come out of seclusion until she had calmed down. When she kept screaming anyway, two beefy security guards were summoned. They stood around her threatening to restrain her if she didn't quit yelling.

Even though I was feeling desperate myself, I didn't like the way this woman was being treated, so my heart went out to her. But when I got up to try and talk to her, one of the security guards admonished me by telling me to sit back down. But I was feeling worse every minute. My friend Joe brought me to the hospital around ten a.m, but I ended up having to wait in E.R. for nearly six hours.

Finally, a nurse approached me to say I needed to have an EKG. After that was taken care of, I was escorted to the psych ward on the third floor of the hospital. I felt a mix of dread and relief; dread because I had never been admitted to the psych ward before, and relief that I was finally getting the help I needed.

Around five in the afternoon, I was ushered into the locked ward of the unit. There a psych aide led me into a small room where he told me to take off my belt, untie my shoelaces, and surrender my backpack. He explained this was necessary so I wouldn't hurt myself. He added that my things would be stored in a locker for safekeeping while I was in the unit. If I needed them, I'd have to ask for permission at the nurse's desk. Then I had to empty my pockets to make sure I had nothing sharp in them. I also had to hand over my wallet, checkbook, and apartment keys. After I'd emptied my pockets, the aide explained how the code system worked. Codes 1 and 2 were for those who needed to stay in the locked ward. Code 3 meant that you could leave the unit if accompanied by a staff person. And Code 4 meant you could leave for a few hours to retrieve some things from home, go out for a walk, or get a bite to eat in the hospital cafeteria. Initially, every newly admitted patient was on Codes 1 and 2. After they got more stable, they earned the right to graduate to Codes 3 and 4. Often this necessitated a doctor's permission. Even when patients were cleared to leave, they needed to sign out at the nurse's desk.

Once all the preliminaries were taken care of, I was escorted into a large dayroom in the middle of the unit. There I saw about a dozen other patients sitting in several armchairs, a sofa, and around a table. One person was busy working on a jigsaw puzzle. A couple of others were playing cards. One man kept pacing back and forth while holding onto a stuffed animal that resembled a duck. He told me its name was Quacky. A skinny woman in her late thirties named Yvonne sat in a rocking chair in one corner of the room rocking back and forth while cradling a doll baby in her arms. She never said a word. A chubby woman named Lisa reminded me of one of the Turnaround residents who had multiple personalities. When I asked her name, she replied, "Today, I'm Carmen." Another young woman paced nervously back and forth in a small adjoining room. Its walls were padded and there was no other furniture. The door had a small window on top. I figured that the staff had put her in seclusion like the woman I had seen in E.R.

Scared and overwhelmed, I wondered how I would spend the rest of that weekend since I was admitted late on a Friday afternoon, and there was no program all day Saturday or Sunday. But I was pleasantly surprised to see three people in the unit that I recognized from other parts of my life. One woman named Mary had been my big sister at Turnaround where I had lived in some fifteen years before. Another named Jane, I knew from a mental health drop-in center I was a member of. And the third person was a woman named Casey who had worked with me twenty years ago as a waitress in the pizza restaurant where I had my first job after moving to Minnesota. It was very comforting to meet people I could talk to. Otherwise, it would have been a long weekend.

As I gradually got acclimated to the ward, I became aware of the nursing station on one side of the room. From there a nurse handed out medications to the patients in the evening. She also doled out cups of coffee and tea. One woman kept going there to have another cup of coffee about every half hour. Finally, the nurse on duty told that she had had enough. Occasionally, I heard the woman in the seclusion room yell out obscenities. I overheard from one of the men playing cards that she was court ordered to be here, something about a Jarvis procedure, and that she was destined to be committed to a state hospital after she left the unit. He told me she had had tried to kill herself shortly before being admitted.

Since I hadn't eaten for about six hours when I was admitted, I asked the nurse if I could take some of the money from my wallet to buy candy and a soft drink from the vending machine on one corner of the room. After she gave me permission, I quickly grabbed a can of coke and a Hershey bar. No sooner had I had sat down to finish my candy bar, than an aide summoned me to meet with my psychiatrist, Dr. Bousahoff, who worked in the hospital.

Dr. Bousahoff had been my doctor for about six months. He was assigned to me while I was attending the day-treatment program prior to being hospitalized. But I never really liked the man. He was very stiff and formal, always referring to me as Mr. Wentersdorf, never by my first name. He had put me on Prozac and Gabapentin to deal with my depression and anxiety. Now he told me that he would be seeing me every couple of days to see how I was doing. He would decide if I needed any change in my medications. After asking me if I had any suicidal ideation, he upped my dosage of Prozac from 25 to 50 milligrams, and added two new medications I had never heard of before called Effexor and Busbar. He assured me that these plus the Gabapentin I was already on, should relieve the depression and anxiety I was feeling. Then he told me he would like to see me again in a couple of days to see how I was responding to the meds.

Although I was very leery about the possible side effects of all these drugs, I was afraid to ask Dr. Bousahoff to change his prescriptions. I had never wanted to see a doctor in the first place, but the day-treatment staff insisted that in order to be in the program I had to see a psychiatrist and go on meds. And he was the one they assigned me to.

It wasn't long before I started feeling the side effects of the new prescriptions. Even though I was already nervous and jumpy before being hospitalized, I now started to feel as if I was crawling out of my skin. My mouth became as dry as sandpaper, so that I kept having to drink water every few minutes. At the same time, urinating became more and more difficult. Plus, I became severely constipated. In fact, I only had one bowel movement the entire time I was in the unit. This was due not only in reaction to the meds, but also because of the starchy food they served, plus the lack of exercise. My vision became blurry, and I felt woozy and lethargic. At night I got the chills because the blanket they gave me wasn't warm enough.

Saturday and Sunday seemed to drag on forever. Not only was there nothing to do to relieve the boredom, but I sorely missed getting any exercise, especially the daily walks I was used to taking. I spent a lot of time pacing back and forth in the dayroom. I found a stationary bike in one corner of the room which I used for about a half an hour twice a day. I played a lot of solitaire. When I tried reading the book I'd brought along, I found it almost impossible to focus, but kept reading the same sentence over and over again.

Fortunately, there was some relief on Saturday evening when some aides took us to a heated, therapeutic pool in the basement of the hospital. I was able to move around in the warm water for about an hour which calmed my jangled nerves. That felt so good and helped counteract some of the side effects the meds were causing.

II

As hard as it was getting through those first few days, the nights were even worse. Because of the new drugs I was on and the unfamiliar surroundings, I hardly got any sleep. As I tossed and turned, I kept ruminating on all the things that had happened before I was admitted. My depression and anxiety had worsened during the past six months, despite being in day-treatment. I remembered the suicidal thoughts and panic attacks that had kept me awake at night. Even seeing an individual therapist every other week was no longer helping. In fact, the last time I saw her, I got very angry because she told me that I had gotten into a cycle of negative thinking that kept me stuck.

As I tried to fall asleep, I fantasized about ways to kill myself. Would it be by jumping from my 10th floor apartment window like that guy who jumped from the 20th floor of my building onto the concrete pavement below last summer? Or like the U of M college professor and poet John Berryman who leapt into the Mississippi River from the Washington Avenue Bridge some twenty years ago? Or would it be like that woman from Turnaround who died of drug overdose fifteen years ago? But I realized that there was no painless way to die. What was even scarier was to think of never waking up again.

In my mind, I kept ruminating about how hard it had been these past few months doing the things I normally loved, like listening to music, writing in my journal, reading, or talking to friends. I worried about all the phone messages that were accumulating on my answering machine. But I was too scared to answer my phone. The despair I felt was so overwhelming that all I wanted to do was sleep. When I finally did force myself to get up around noon each day, I spent endless hours playing video games on my computer, like hearts, spider solitaire, and cribbage. In the evening I watched TV until late at night. I subsisted on chips and canned food. I hardly ever showered, shaved, or brushed my teeth. My apartment was a complete mess with dishes stacked in the sink, dust on all the furniture, and papers and unanswered mail scattered everywhere. Plus, I had to face an apartment inspection in a couple of weeks. I dreaded leaving my apartment for fear of running into people. Going grocery shopping was agonizing because I had to deal with salesclerks and other customers. Furthermore, I felt so overwhelmed by all the stuff on the shelves, that I couldn't decide what to buy.

Just before my depression kicked in, I had become so overextended with all kinds of activities and commitments that I couldn't keep up with them all. There was a church concert I was scheduled to play at a week from Monday. Then there was a storytelling gig I was supposed to attend on Friday. And a community ed harmonica class I was due to teach next month. I remembered how I just barely got through hosting a monthly Open Stage at my church the night before I was hospitalized. When I asked Joe to sub for me because I just couldn't do it, he persuaded me to go anyway, and came along to offer me support. Summoning every bit of will power I possessed, I forced myself to show up. I was pleasantly surprised at how well things went. We had a near record turnout, and I managed to get through the evening O.K. But as soon as I got home, the depression hit me again like a sledgehammer, so that I could hardly move out of bed! That night I had a horrible nightmare about flinging myself under a speeding freight train. Finally, around five or six Sunday morning, I was finally able to doze off for a couple of hours before breakfast. But when I did get up, I was so groggy I could hardly keep my eyes open the rest of the day.

III

Sunday afternoon, I got my first visitors. One of them was a former pastor at my church who now worked as a hospital chaplain. She led me in a few prayers and encouraged me to call her once I got out of the hospital. My friend Joe came to see how I was doing and asked me if I needed anything. Some people came from church, as well as a woman I'd gotten to know at Turnaround, who brought along her mom. It was comforting to have outside people to talk to. When I told them of the problems I was having with my meds, they urged me to talk to my doctor about it, and if he didn't respond, to ask for a second opinion. Joe told me I was in charge of my treatment, and the doctors were there to serve me, not the other way around.

On Sunday night I still got hardly any sleep. When I saw Dr. Bousahoff again Monday morning, I complained to him about the side effects the meds were having, especially my problems sleeping. He told me that I needed to be on the new dosages he had prescribed because of my suicidal ideation. Moreover, he added 50 milligrams of Trazedone to help me sleep. He also upped my daily dose of Gabapentin to 200 milligrams. The following night I was finally able to get some sleep, but I didn't like the way the Trazedone knocked me out. That night I had no dreams, but the next morning I still felt drowsy, as if someone had put my head in a vise. On Monday morning after breakfast the regular hospital program began. But first I was seen by a medical doctor who checked my vital signs, examined my head, heart, and stomach.

Fortunately, he didn't find anything wrong with me physically. When I complained to him about my constipation and problems urinating, he urged me to tell my psychiatrist about that. I felt as if I was caught in a Catch 22 situation.

After seeing the doctor, I attended some of the daily activities. I gradually became comfortable with the hospital routine. At 9:00 a.m. there was a community meeting where I met with all the staff people working with me: my case worker, a nurse, an occupational therapist, my primary therapist, and a psych aide. When I complained about the side effects my meds were causing, my therapist suggested that I get a second opinion. She encouraged me to make an appointment with the in-patient hospital psychiatrist, Dr. Vandemere who was scheduled to come to the unit on Tuesday morning. At the end of the meeting, my case worker suggested I set a goal for the rest of the week. Then she asked, "What is your favorite day of the week? And why?"

After thinking about that for a minute, I replied, "Sunday, because I always look forward to attending church."

At 10:00 a.m. there was a verbal group. This was a kind of therapy group, like the one I attended in the day-treatment program, except that there were fewer people. I really liked my group therapist Emily whom I found very warm and encouraging. She began the group by asking each of us what was our favorite thing to do at home. When I said I loved to play music, she asked me if I wanted to bring in my guitar sometime while I was in the unit to play a song for everyone. I told her that would really be neat.

Then we started the serious business of therapy. Yvonne, the woman who held the doll baby in her rocking chair, and hadn't said a word so far, finally opened up. She spoke about the abuse she had suffered as a child. She said she had been raped by her uncle and grandfather, and that her mother, who knew about the abuse, had refused to intervene. The man with Quacky the duck talked about hearing Satanic voices that told him to jump off a bridge. Everyone shared something about their lives. I waited until last because I was scared to speak up. But finally, with Emily's encouragement, I took the plunge.

Emily asked me what had brought me to the hospital. So, I talked about my depression and anxiety while describing my symptoms such as playing computer games all day, not answering my phone, watching too much TV, staying in bed until late in the morning, and wishing I was dead. Then she surprised me by adding: "But what do you think triggered your suicidal thoughts?"

At first, I couldn't think of what had brought on my recent crisis. But then, as soon as I started talking, ideas popped into my head, things I hadn't even thought about before.

"While I was growing up, my dad employed this German lady to be our housekeeper since my mom had died when I was young. She did the cleaning and cooking for us, and my dad used to call her Twinkletoes , but her real name was Paula. Well, shortly before Christmas, I visited Paula, her husband, and her two kids in Phoenix. She revealed some things about me and my dad that I hadn't known before. For example, she told me that she used to be very concerned about me while I was growing up because I was so painfully shy. She also wondered why I never allowed her to get close. She noticed that I was very protective of my dad who, she told me, was often very demanding."

I continued, "After visiting Paula and her family, I traveled to San Francisco to see my dad for Christmas. When I told him about my talk with Paula, he got angry with me because he thought I was blaming him for my shyness and inability to open up. He didn't think it was right for me to talk about him with her, that it was none of my business. After that exchange, the rest of my visit was very tense, and my dad didn't speak of the matter again. When I got back home, I tried in vain to repress my feelings."

"It makes a lot of sense why your two visits would trigger a major crisis in your life," Emily replied. "There's probably a lot of buried stuff between you and your dad that neither of you have ever dealt with. I would encourage you to talk more about this in therapy. I think it would help you heal your childhood hurts."

After Emily's supportive feedback, I felt a huge wave of relief. For the first time since I had been hospitalized, I felt hopeful, determined to talk about these things in the future. The rest of the day went much better. After lunch and a short break during which I took a much-needed nap, there was a therapeutic recreation group in which the recreational therapist Susan passed out paper, magic markers, and crayons, and asked us to draw. Since a few people didn't know what to draw, she gave them sheets of paper filled with circular, black-and-white Mandalas which she encouraged them to color in. I found that drawing really calmed my nerves. After dinner, I was able to go swimming again in the therapeutic pool. That night after taking my Trazedone, I was finally able to get a good night's sleep.

The next day when Dr. Vandemere made his rounds, I asked for permission to see him. This was very hard for me even though both Joe and my therapist had encouraged me to get a second opinion. I was convinced that Dr. Vandemere would get mad at me for questioning Dr. Bousahoff's prescriptions. I figured that all the doctors were in cahoots with one another.

However, Dr. Vandemere seemed much more approachable than Dr. Bousahoff. He was a tall, friendly looking man in his late fifties with a full beard and a gentle smile. There was a twinkle in his eye that suggested he had a good sense of humor. He also walked with a slight limp. That made him seem less threatening and more vulnerable which I took as a good sign. So, taking a deep breath, I plunged ahead. I told him about my constipation and problems urinating, as well the wooziness and chills. I was pleasantly surprised that he didn't get defensive. He also told me that Dr. Bousahoff had interned with him ten years ago, and that they were still in touch. He encouraged me to talk with Dr. Bousahoff at my next meeting, and to be honest with him about the negative side effects of my medications. He assured me that he would be willing to listen.

Then he asked me to tell him a little bit about myself and what had brought me to the hospital. From the way he listened to me, I got the sense that he was genuinely concerned about my welfare.

"From what I heard you say, I'm convinced that your depression is the result of the multiple losses and changes in your life over which you had no control. These include your early abandonment by your birth mom, your time in the orphanage, the loss of your adoptive mom, your many moves, your emigration to the U.S., and your time in foster homes. Any one of these would have been enough to trigger a depressive episode."

Even though I was very hopeful after talking with Dr. Vandemere, I was disappointed at his insistence that I stay on the meds Dr. Bousahoff had prescribed until I talked with him again.

"Because of the frequent recurrence of your depression, I'm convinced that you need to be on some kinds of prescription meds for the rest of your life. I firmly believe that any other psychiatrist you might choose to work with would feel the same way. He might try some different meds to counter your current side effects, or change some of the dosages, but you'll need to stay on some kinds of meds permanently in order to prevent another episode like the one that brought you to the hospital."

Discouraged by Dr. Vandemere's assessment because it wasn't what I had hoped for, I made one more attempt to suggest an alternative to the meds. I told him that one of my friends had suggested I try out some wholistic, homeopathic remedies like St. John's Wort because they were supposedly effective in counteracting depression, but without the debilitating side effects of prescription drugs. I also told him about the body work I had found so helpful at Turnaround like Yoga, T'ai Chi, and bioenergetics.

"I don't know anything about bioenergetics, Tony. And I don't think that new age practices like Yoga or T'ai Chi can deal with clinical depression. I think that some of the more extreme practices tried in the 70s like scream therapy, anger reduction, and rebirthing have been discredited. As for herbal remedies like St. John's Wort, they are only known to work for people with mild symptoms. But your kind of long-term, recurring, clinical depression is much more serious. In people like yourself, only prescription meds have been scientifically proven to be effective. And even their use isn't an exact science, but is subject to continual change, depending on current medical research. However, I urge you for now to follow Dr. Bousahoff's advice since I find him to be very capable."

After my conversation with Dr. Vandemere, I felt discouraged, but didn't want to press the issue about continuing on my meds. I thought that I could seek out a new psychiatrist once I returned to the day-treatment program.

IV

As the rest week went by, I got more and more comfortable in the hospital, all except for the doctors' visits. I even found myself looking forward to the various groups, especially the verbal group with Emily. I also enjoyed attending Susan's therapeutic recreation group. She brought in lots of creative ideas that kept us engaged. One day, for example, she introduced us to a kind of mindfulness meditation during which she asked us to close our eyes while she played some soothing music. She asked us to focus on our breathing while imagining what our favorite day would be like. I imagined myself to be on the ocean shore in Virginia Beach where I frolicked in the waves, basked in the sunshine, and curled my toes into the sand while walking along the beach. I was able to get into my fantasy so much that I nodded off for a few minutes.

During the week, I also got a visit from my current church pastor, Kurt, who had been the director of Turnaround. When I told him about my suicidal thoughts, he asked me if I blamed God for of all the pain I had suffered. I told him I had never thought about it like that.

"It's O.K. to be angry at God, even rageful," he said. "Because God can handle anything you might throw at Him. Think of the prophet Jeremiah in the Old Testament. He raged against God, yet wasn't punished for it. God is more understanding of your pain than you might think. Furthermore, I don't think that God is a vengeful deity who intentionally inflicts pain on anyone. Most of the evil in the world is caused by other human beings. And depression, as you know, is a clinical illness which is not your fault. However, I do believe that God can help relieve your suffering if you just lean on Him in prayer. You also need to learn to accept your illness instead of fighting it. I highly recommend a book that helped me deal with my own doubts and faith struggles. It is written by Thomas Moore and is called *Care of the Soul*. Reading Moore's book really helped me deal with my son's suicide when he was sixteen. In fact, if it hadn't been for my faith, I don't know what I would have done."

I was buoyed up by Kurt's visit. As the week progressed, my depression gradually began to lift. I started feeling better about being in the hospital, in large part because of all the support I was getting. A day after I saw Kurt, I got another visit from Dr. Bousahoff. Although I didn't tell him that I had talked with Dr. Vandemere, I did say I was feeling better. I also reiterated some of my concerns, especially the constipation and urination problems. Fortunately, he didn't react as negatively as I had feared, but offered to lower my dose of Effexor. Otherwise, he thought that my body would gradually adjust to my meds. Because I was still uncomfortable around him, I didn't press him any further.

By Thursday, I was feeling confident enough to ask permission to leave the hospital for a couple of hours to take a walk. That way I could finally get the exercise I'd been craving all week. Emily gave me permission to go on Code 4, so I could leave the premises for a while. Thus, I signed out after recreational therapy group and promised to get back in time for dinner. It felt so good to be outside again for the first time in five days. Even though it was a bit blustery, I took a long walk along the banks of the Mississippi which flowed near the hospital grounds. Just feeling the wind on my cheeks and getting my legs moving gave me a lift. By the time I got back about an hour later, I even had an appetite.

Friday was my last day in the hospital. I had another community meeting with my group therapist, recreational therapist, and case worker. They decided that I was ready to leave the hospital that day if I wanted to. Emily suggested that once I left the in-patient unit I return to my day-treatment program three days a week. That way I could continue working on some of the issues that came up while I was an in-patient. This was a great relief because I had begun to worry about how I was going to get support once I was on my own again. In fact, I had gone from dreading being in the hospital, to being afraid to leave.

On Friday afternoon, I experienced the best group yet. It was a spiritual life group led by a minister named Peter. The group was fairly small, only four people, so each person got plenty of time to share. Pastor Peter asked us some of the same questions that Kurt had asked me – whether people were angry at God and believed that God had caused their pain. One woman named Sandra told us that she had rejected her Catholic faith as a teenager and was now an agnostic. A man named John said that he heard voices that kept telling him he was evil. He believed the voices were sent by Satan to punish him for his sins. I mentioned that I felt a lot of guilt and shame, especially because of my sexual urges, since I was taught that masturbation was a mortal sin punishable by an eternity in hell.

After listening to the people in the group, Pastor Peter read a Bible passage from Job as well as some of the Psalms. Then he urged us to counter our negative thoughts by replacing them with healing ones. He also encouraged us to use prayer and affirmations to put us in a positive frame of mind. At the end of the session, he led us in a creative visualization exercise in which we were to imagine being held in the arms of a loving God, however we imagined that God to be. After that group, I felt a deep sense of peace.

Late Friday afternoon, I finally said goodbye to the people I'd gotten to know in the course of the week, including two of my friends who were still there. I also said goodbye to Emily, my recreational therapist Susan, my case worker, and Pastor Peter. Emily encouraged me to keep working in day-treatment on the issues surrounding my dad.

One of the aides then handed me back my belt, shoelaces, apartment keys, wallet, and backpack. My case worker took me downstairs to where the day-treatment program was located, so I could sign up for the following week. That way I could prevent another relapse. I was very fortunate that my friend Joe offered to pick me up from the hospital that evening. He not only treated me to dinner at a nearby Perkins restaurant, but offered to drive me home afterwards.

My first night back home was very strange. I felt as if I was a visitor in my own apartment. It seemed like an eternity since I'd been there last. I deliberately didn't turn on the TV so I could reflect on all the things I had experienced. It was comforting to know that I could continue to attend the day-treatment program where I could keep working on the issues I uncovered in the hospital. I also resolved to do my best to find another psychiatrist. I hoped I could get a referral from my day-treatment therapist. And before going to sleep, I marveled at how much things had changed for me in just one short week. From being scared to go into the hospital, I'd gotten to the point that I missed being there. My depression no longer weighed me down. I felt a new ray of hope.

PART III

MY LIFE WITH MUSIC

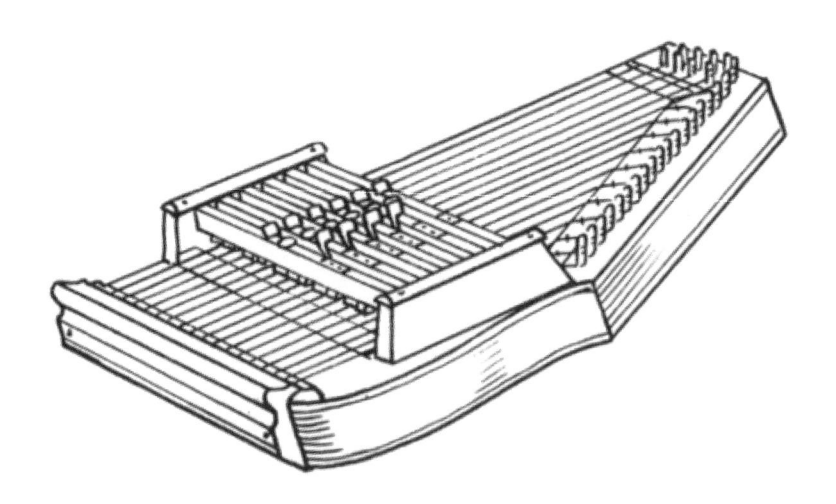

PART III

MY LIFE WITH MUSIC

I

Music makes the world go 'round,
I just need some happy sounds
To brighten up my nights and days.
Music makes the world go 'round,
If I'm lost, I can be found
With these songs to show me the way.
There are moments that I'd like to keep,
Every night before I go to sleep.
Music makes the world go 'round,
Some songs silly, some profound,
Some can make me laugh and play.
Music makes the world go 'round,
Keeps my spirits off the ground,
Makes me want to sing and play.
There are times I feel I want to die,
But then I hear a melody go by.
Music, sweet music,
Music, sweet music, don't go away.

I was born in 1945 in Marburg an der Lahn, a sleepy university town in Germany about 50 kilometers north of Frankfurt am Main. As a baby, I was often soothed to sleep by the sweet strains of Brahms' famous lullaby.

> *Guten Abend, gute Nacht, mit Rosen bedacht,*
> *Mit Naeglein besteckt, schluepf unter die Deck,'*
> *Morgen frueh, wenn Gott will, wirst Du wieder geweckt,*
> *Morgen frueh, wenn Gott will, wirst Du wieder geweckt.*

Good evening, goodnight, with roses bedight,
With your nails small and white, we bid you goodnight,
In the morning, if God wills, you will wake up again,
In the morning when God wills, you will wake up again.

As a little boy, I heard lots of music all around me. However, some of the children's songs back then were a far cry from Raffi, Sesame Street, or Mister Rogers. Here's one I remember distinctly.

> *Fuchs, Du hast die Gans gestohlen,*
> *Gib sie wieder her, gib sie wieder her,*
> *Sonst wird dich der Jaeger holen mit dem Schiessgewehr,*
> *Sonst wird dich der jaeger holen mit them Schiessgewehr.*

O you fox, you stole the goose,
Give it back again, give it back again,
Or the hunter, he will shoot you,
With his gun and then.

While I was growing up in Germany, my dad loved to listen to classical music. He acquired some of the first long-playing records that appeared in the 1950s. I recall that he owned almost all the Beethoven symphonies conducted by Arturo Toscanini. I grew up listening to melodies like the famous *Ode to Joy*.

After I moved to the U.S., and I was around eleven, my dad initiated my musical education. He introduced me to Prokovieff's famous children's tone poem *Peter and the Wolf*, which featured characters like a grandfather, a wolf, a goose, and a hunter. All of them were introduced by different orchestral instruments like bassoon, oboe, and tympani.

When I was fourteen, my dad bought an old used upright piano that had once been a player piano. Because he knew that I was interested in music, he set up piano lessons for me with our church organist Helen Gough. Every Saturday morning I dutifully hiked to Miss Gough's home in Cincinnati for my weekly piano lesson. There I learned to play classical piano exercises by Clementi, as well as sonatinas by Bach, Mozart, and Beethoven. I remember some of my favorite pieces included Eric Sati's *Gymnopedie*, Beethoven's *Fuer Elise* and *Moonlight Sonata*, Mozart's *Turkish Rondo*, Bach's *Well Tempered Klavier*, and Debussy's *Claire de Lune*. However, because I didn't always practice the pieces I was supposed to, preferring instead to improvise my own tunes, my dad eventually got rid of the piano.

That was unfortunate, but I was still able to play music since, around that time, I joined my junior high school marching band where I learned to play the flute. There I was first introduced to Sousa marches and more popular music.

By the time I started college at Xavier University in 1964, I joined the X.U. marching band where I took up the flute again. During the fall and winter, I played for college football and basketball games. In the spring, I continued in the concert band. At Xavier, I not only played march tunes, but also selections from movies, musicals, show tunes, and some classical compositions. I remember our band playing the theme song from the James Bond film *Goldfinger*. Another piece that made a big impression on me was the overture to Leonard Bernstein's opera *Candide*.

It was also at Xavier that I was introduced to a whole different kind of music, thanks to my dorm roommate Gene. I started listening to rock-n-roll music on Cincinnati's top 40s stations such as WUBE and WSAI. There I discovered the world of '60s rock-n-roll with groups like The Beatles, Rolling Stones, Mamas and Papas, The Doors, Beach Boys, Bee Gees, Sonny and Cher, Simon and Garfunkel, the Byrds, and the Monkees. I also fell in love with individual singers like Dylan and Neil Diamond.

While attending grad school at Ohio State in the fall of 1968, I lived in a dorm where I continued to listen to top forties rock-n-roll. But at that time, I fell in love with a woman who introduced me to the folk music of Judy Collins, Joan Baez, and Peter, Paul and Mary. In the spring of 1969, she persuaded me to take folk guitar lessons. I learned to play the songs of Dylan, Paul Simon, Tom Paxton, Donovan, Phil Ochs, and John Denver. Two of that year's musical highlights included attending concerts by Peter, Paul, and Mary, and Doc Watson.

When I moved back to my hometown Marburg in 1970, I continued to play my guitar. I also added the harmonica so I could play ala Dylan. I'll never forget the thrill I got when I first heard John Denver's *Rocky Mountain High* and Cat Stevens' *Moon Shadow*. While living in a student dorm I also discovered the songs of Woodie Guthrie as well as some old-time and bluegrass records.

It was in 1971 that I began writing my own songs. One of them, called *Bear with Me, My Friend*, starts out:

Bear with me, my friend, don't strike me out,

Observe all these changes, within to without,

First, tell me your name, so I may find,

You really are nothing, but what's in your mind.

In 1974, after moving to Minneapolis, my music took me in lots of different directions. In the next forty years my horizons expanded to include country, gospel, classic rock, and jazz. I learned to play new instruments such as the autoharp, mountain dulcimer, fiddle, tin whistle, accordion, and ukulele. I also began teaching guitar, harmonica, tin whistle, and autoharp at various Minneapolis community schools.

During this time, I started playing music at Open Mics, coffeehouses, nursing homes, and churches. From 1988 to 2008, I hosted a monthly open stage at Walker Community Church in South Minneapolis. There I recorded my first two albums of original songs. Later I recorded more CDs with my singing partner Mary while playing a variety of instruments. And on Sunday mornings I often played my autoharp, harmonica, and tin whistle at the Walker church service, at least until the pandemic put everything on hold. Yes, music has always been a vital part of my life and will continue to be so for many years to come.

II

Thank you, dad, for saving me from a life of endless sorrow,
Thank you, dad, for giving me a new home, a new tomorrow,
Thank you, dad, for staying there when others had all gone,
Thank you, dad, for teaching me to be wise and strong.
Whenever I hear a line from a Shakespeare play,
My long night's journey turns back into day,
Whenever Butterfly is singing Un Bel Die,
I think of you and wonder what could be.
You lived a life both long and full of promise and regrets,
Survived the thirties and the war, wanting to forget.
You lost your wife and Germany, and made yourself anew,
But never gave up the will to live, and made your dreams come true.
And now that you have passed away, and your soul's at rest.
I think of all those people who by your life were blessed.
I'm glad we both drew closer and left our pain behind,
To walk together hand in hand and ease our troubled minds.

A few years ago, I saw a magnificent production of Giaccomo Puccini's final opera, *Turandot*. Hearing and seeing it with friends from church transported me to my teens, and made me think of my dad because it was one of his favorite operas. The beautiful Ordway concert hall was packed to capacity, a tribute to the excellence of the production, since the performance took place on an off-day in the middle of the week. And the artists singing the roles were all alternates. Yet I found myself so moved that when the curtain finally came down, I jumped to my feet to clap and join the thunderous applause of appreciation for such a great performance.

My journey towards the world of opera was a long and circuitous one. The year before I saw *Turandot*, I heard a wonderful rendition of another one of my dad's favorite operas, *Madame Butterfly*, at the same theater. I also found it very moving, especially since I heard it just a few months after my dad's funeral.

I was first introduced to the world of opera around the age of twelve in 1957. At that time, my dad's closest friend, Arnold Euler, emigrated from Germany to the U.S. My dad was his sponsor. Arnold stayed with us for about a year until he could find an apartment of his own. He was in his late twenties at the time and had a fine tenor voice. In fact, his dream was to become an opera singer. I'll never forget listening to the old, scratchy Enrico Caruso records he brought to our Volkert Place apartment. Both he and my dad shared a love of opera. They spent many hours listening to my dad's recordings of Verdi, Wagner, and Puccini. They had gotten to know each other back in Germany where my dad was living in the home of Arnold's parents. There my dad had introduced Arnold, who was fifteen years younger, to the world of grand opera. My dad even coached Arnold in Italian pronunciation.

Now, living in Cincinnati, Arnold decided to pursue his opera singing dream by enrolling at the prestigious Cincinnati Conservatory of Music where one of my dad's friends was teaching voice, and where Arnold enrolled in classes of voice and opera performance. I can still recall him joining my dad to sing their favorite Puccini arias such as *Nessun Dorma* from *Turandot*, *Che Gelida Manina* from *La Boheme*, *Visi d'Arte* from *Tosca*, and *Un Bel Die* from *Madame Butterfly*. As a matter of fact, the running joke between them was that Arnold was destined to become the next German tenor singing sensation: *Arnoldo Wiesecko*.

Unfortunately, Arnold soon gave up his opera singing dream in order to pursue the more practical career of an offset printer. He gradually worked his way up to foreman at a large Cincinnati printing plant where he became friends with another German immigrant and his family. Eventually, Arnold went back to Germany to marry his boyhood sweetheart, Hannelore. He brought her back to the States. For a while, they stayed at my dad's new home near the Xavier University campus. As soon as Arnold was earning enough, he and Hannelore moved into an apartment of their own in a Cincinnati suburb, where my dad and I would often visit, especially on Christmas and New Year's. Every now and then, Arnold would bring out his violin to play some classical pieces, or he would sing opera arias with my dad. But he never pursued his opera career dream again.

My dad's love of opera never flagged. Even when swamped with his new responsibilities as a college professor of English literature, such as giving lectures, preparing exams, grading papers, or doing research, he always found time to listen to his favorite operas such as Wagner's *Tristan und Isolde*, Richard Strauss' *Salome*, and Puccini's *Turandot*. Although he hardly ever listened to the radio, every Saturday afternoon he would tune in the Texaco sponsored live weekly New York Metropolitan Opera broadcasts. Since I became bored with opera music during my teen years, the favorite part of the broadcast was always the opera quiz which was hosted during intermissions by Rudolf Bing. These featured interviews with famous opera stars, as well as interesting facts about various opera performances. A few times, my dad and I even headed for the Cincinnati Zoo where the Cincinnati Opera Company held live performances to the accompaniment of chimpanzees and orangutangs.

As I grew older, I abandoned my interest in opera. In college, for example, I was burning to discover my own kind of music. Now, when my dad played his opera records, I tuned them out, especially those interminably long passages from Wagner's *Ring* cycle like *Die Walkuere, Das Rheingold,* and *Goetterdaemmerung* during which hefty, horned women belted out endless arias with their screechy sopranos that left me cold.

At first, I turned to the modern classical music of composers like Antheil, Shostokovich, Bartok, and Stravinsky. But soon I fell in love with top forties rock-n-roll. Now, I was listening to the Beatles' *Sargent Pepper's Lonely Heart's Club Band*, and Simon and Garfunkel's *Sounds of Silence*, not Wagner's *Ride of the Valkyries*. After graduating from college, my musical horizons widened even more to include folk music, blues, bluegrass, gospel, country, and jazz.

But eventually, I did return to my classical roots. I resumed listening to the favorite composers of my childhood like Beethoven, Brahms, Dvorak, Tchaikovsky, and Mahler. Eventually, I even resumed listening to my old opera favorites. This enthusiasm increased even more after my dad's death. My one regret is that I never got a chance to hear some of my dad's old favorites with him.

However, while listening to *Madame Butterfly, Tosca, La Boheme*, and *Turandot* at the Ordway, I once again felt a powerful connection with my dad. Hearing that passionate music transported me back to my childhood when my dad would regale me with stories of how he and my mom attended the Berliner Staatsoper in the 1930s and 1940s to hear Renate Tebaldi or Kirsten Flagstad sing Puccini and Wagner.

While listening to *Turandot*, seeing the grand pageantry of this magnificent production with its stunning costumes and its imaginative staging, I could almost sense my dad sitting next to me. I acquired a deeper insight into his character. I realized that there was more to him than an intellectual scholar who lived primarily in his head. By sharing his love of opera with me, I was able to witness the passion in his soul. And I'm thankful for that.

III

Everybody wants to be a star
When they play on stage.
No matter who they are
They want their fifteen minutes worth of fame.
Strings are strummed,
And drums are drummed,
As they hope they'll be
The next Cat or Joan, or Bob.
Then it's over till next week,
Or next month,
Or not at all.

My first open stage was so traumatic that I didn't attend another one until five years later. It all took place in the winter of 1975 before I knew anything about autoharps. At the time I was playing mostly songs by Bob Dylan, Cat Stevens, Paul Simon, Tom Paxton, and John Denver on my guitar and harmonica. This open stage took place one Sunday a month at The Whole Coffeehouse in the basement of Coffman Union on the University of Minnesota campus. On Friday and Saturday evenings, the Whole featured national folk music acts like Odetta, Tom Paxton, Sonny and Terry, and John Fahey. Sundays were open stage nights.

When I arrived at The Whole that winter evening in 1975, I was an hour early so I could be sure to get a chance to play. There were already about a dozen performers with their guitars sitting at the round wooden tables bedecked with candles. I was nervous because this was my first open stage, and I didn't know what to expect.

About half an hour before the music started, the emcee showed up. He was a young, corpulent man wearing a ten-gallon hat. He told the would-be performers to put their names into his hat, while warning us that some people wouldn't get a chance to play because there wasn't enough time to accommodate everyone. We would be chosen at random. Then he went into this lengthy spiel about how performers, to be effective, should not only be talented, but also project confidence, have good audience rapport, and stage presence. By the time he had finished, I was really shaking in my boots.

As the evening wore on and each performer played their three songs, I became more and more flustered, hoping that my name wouldn't be drawn, so I wouldn't have to face the audience. But towards the end of the evening around 11 p.m., I heard the emcee call my name, except he got it wrong. "Tony Winterdrop, you're up next."

As I slowly made my way onto the stage, my guitar and harmonica in hand, my hands were already shaking. By this time there were only about half a dozen people left in the audience. The room was completely dark, and I was blinded by the spotlight on my face. With trembling fingers, I launched into my first song, Cat Stevens' *The Wind*. I followed it with two other songs I don't even remember. I was so nervous that I was completely oblivious to the audience. I just wanted to get this ordeal over with as fast as I could. I certainly didn't notice if there was any applause.

Finally, after an agonizing ten minutes, I managed to stumble off the stage to slink back to my seat, avoiding any eye contact with others, glad this was over. I hung my head in shame and embarrassment, resolving never to return any time soon. After this traumatic experience, I made up my mind that if I ever hosted an open stage, I wouldn't do it like that guy with the hat. On the contrary, I'd encourage the performers on stage by making them feel as comfortable as I could.

And, sure enough, when I did have a chance to host my own open stage at Walker Church 13 years later in the fall of 1988, I did just that. And I continued hosting for the next 20 years.

IV

I want an autoharp for Christmas,
I can strum my blues away.
I want to learn those old-time ballads
That Mother Maybelle used to play,
And wile away the winter hours,
With Yuletide carols warm and bright,
Like Jingle Bells and Hark the Herald,
What Child Is This and Silent Night.

I want an autoharp for Christmas,
Just give me any model, please,
Chromatic or diatonic,
So, I can pick those melodies.
I'll play my heart on three octaves,
My fingers flying o'er the strings,
And then I'll tune up for the New Year,
To find out what tomorrow brings.

My love affair with the autoharp began in the winter of 1976. At the time, I was living in a small rooming house in Southeast Minneapolis, not far from KSTP-TV, with seven other international students I met the year before at Namche House, a residence for U of M international students. I had just quit the master's degree program in English as a Second Language, and was now working as a stock clerk at Sears and Roebuck on Chicago and Lake. I spent most of my spare time listening to folk and rock music records

I borrowed from the Minneapolis Public library, or playing my guitar and harmonica.

However, one fortuitous day I discovered an unusual-looking old album entitled *Mountain Music Played on the Autoharp*, which featured three musicians I'd never heard of – Pop Stoneman, Neriah Benfield, and Kilby Snow. They played old-time, country music of the 1930s and 1940s on all kinds of antique-looking autoharps. Up to that time, I had never heard of an autoharp or seen one played. But I checked out the album and brought it home where I played it on my one-speaker stereo. This unusual record immediately became my favorite. I noticed that one of the musicians, Kilby Snow, accompanied his autoharp on the harmonica. At the time I was already playing guitar and harmonica ala Dylan. This old-time music evoked the hollers of Appalachia in West Virginia, Virginia, Kentucky, Tennessee, and North Carolina. The picking was fast and furious, and the voices rough-hewn. I kept renewing the record from the library until I knew every tune by heart.

II

In the course of the next three years, I experienced a series of synchronous events that opened up the world of the autoharp in unexpected ways. In spring 1977, I attended an arts-and-crafts camp for adults near Hudson, Wisconsin called Northlands Rec Lab. We participated in activities like folk dancing, journal writing, and various crafts. We sang songs each morning after breakfast. Our song leader accompanied herself on the autoharp. She showed me how to play a few basic strums and chord progressions. Two years later, when I again attended Rec lab, our song leader was a vivacious, charismatic young woman named Beth who also played the autoharp, but in a much more accomplished way. Since we hit it off, she showed me more autoharp techniques.

About a week after this Rec Lab in spring of 1979, I volunteered at a weekend Minneapolis folk music festival. One evening, I heard a concert in which a talented musician named Bob Zentz played the autoharp, as well as guitar, hammered dulcimer, banjo, and fiddle. Not only did he use the autoharp to accompany himself on songs, but he added instrumental melodies. I was blown away by his virtuosity. At the festival, I also attended an autoharp workshop led by a diminutive young woman named Stevie Beck. She played autoharp instrumentals like fiddle tunes and slip jigs, as well as cowboy songs, and Appalachian ballads. During her concert, she casually mentioned that she gave autoharp lessons at her home. Jumping at the chance to take her up on her offer, I started taking lessons from her that summer.

I always looked forward to my lessons with great enthusiasm. Each week, Stevie wrote out new song arrangements in autoharp tablature. She also taped each lesson so I could learn the new songs at home. Not only was she a great autoharp player, but she was also a good storyteller. One time she told me how she played autoharp at a new live radio show called *The Prairie Home Companion*, hosted by none other than Garrison Keillor. She added that she taught Garrison how to play the autoharp. He returned the favor by billing her as *Queen of the Autoharp* on his show. I took lessons with Stevie for about six months, after which I was ready to venture out on my own. Stevie also helped me pick out my first autoharp because she worked as a luthier at a nearby guitar store.

III

While taking lessons from Stevie, I was working as an activities assistant at a nursing home in North Minneapolis. There I led various music groups for the residents such as sing-a-longs and hymn-sings. I also serenaded the more disabled residents in their rooms. I found out that the autoharp went over much better than the guitar which I had used when I first started this job. Since the residents didn't respond much to the strains of Bob Dylan's *Mr. Tambourine Man*, Leonard Cohen's *Bird on the Wire*, or Paul Simon's *Sounds of Silence*, I had to learn new songs they would appreciate. So, I headed for the library once again, this time to get all the Sing-a-long with Mitch albums I could get my hands on. I learned such popular senior favorites like *Five-Foot-Two, Let me Call You Sweetheart*, and *You Are my Sunshine*.

Two years later, in the spring of 1981, I had a chance to teach my very first community ed class – Autoharp Basics. I was fortunate to have four enthusiastic students, one of whom became a close personal friend, and used the autoharp in the nursing home where she was activities director. Then one year later in the summer of 1982, I got another lucky break. I saw a want ad in a Minneapolis paper that said simply, "Autoharp teacher wanted at the West Bank School of Music." I couldn't believe my good luck! I'd been taking guitar and banjo lessons there for years, yet I never dreamed that I could be teaching there some day. If ever there was a job that was meant for me, this was it! I auditioned and got the job. I found out later that Stevie had taught there before me. I ended up teaching autoharp at the West Bank School of Music for the next ten years.

IV

As the years rolled by, I had a lot of neat experiences with the autoharp. I continued teaching autoharp classes at various Minneapolis community schools. I started subscribing to a wonderful, wacky magazine called *The Autoharpaholic* which featured autoharp arrangements, record reviews, and tips on playing the autoharp. There I published my first arrangement for autoharp. Later, when *The Autoharpaholic* ceased being published, I found another autoharp magazine called *Autoharp Clearinghouse*. I made a neat connection with the editor who not only published more of my autoharp arrangements, but also wrote a profile of me in 1983. It turned out that she and I had a special connection: our mutual German heritage. I ended up sending her autoharp arrangements of German Christmas carols. Unfortunately, the *Autoharp Clearinghouse* also stopped being published after about ten years. But I discovered yet a third autoharp magazine called *Autoharp Quarterly* that published several of my song arrangements as well as two reviews of my CDs.

V

Over the next few years, I lost my autoharp connections. My community ed and West Bank School of Music students dwindled down to nothing. Finally, I lost my WBSM job itself when they hired a new well-known autoharp teacher who had won first place in a national autoharp contest. But eventually, I got back to playing my favorite instrument. Over the next few years, I discovered two music festivals, both of which featured autoharp workshops and contests. One of these –The Walnut Valley Bluegrass Festival– is located in Winfield, Kansas; the other –The Mountain Laurel Autoharp Gathering– is located near Harrisburg, Pennsylvania. I attended both for a number of years, each time competing in their contests. Unfortunately, I was never a finalist, but I had fun trying. There I met a lot of neat autoharp players from all over the country and the world, learned many new techniques in the various workshops, and heard plenty of great autoharp music in the evening concerts.

In the course of the next 40 years, I was also able to record eight CDs of autoharp music and original songs. And in 2005, I founded a local club for autoharp players, the *Twin Cities Autoharpers*. For twelve years, we met once a month at Walker Church in Minneapolis to jam, share songs, and plan events. In this group, I got to know several good friends. Unfortunately, I had to quit hosting this group for personal reasons. But my love of the autoharp has never waned. I still play it at Open Mics, nursing homes, coffeehouses, Walker Church, and whenever an opportunity presents itself. I'm certain that my love affair with the autoharp won't end anytime soon. Indeed, I'm proud to call myself an autoharpaholic!

V

I got them damned old autoharp contest blues,
From the top of my head to the bottom of my shoes,
I never seem to win, but I always lose,
I sure am paying some heavy dues,
With them damned old autoharp contest blues.
I play my heart out each time I compete,
But every time I do, I just get beat.
I never seem to pass the test,
But always end up second best.
I swear to God, my fate is fixed,
I'm either out of tune, or lose my picks,
Each time I play, something goes awry,
It just makes me wanna cry.
I got them damned old autoharp contest blues,
From the top of my head to the bottom of my shoes,
I never seem to win but I always lose,
I sure am paying some heavy dues
With them damned old autoharp contest blues.

I

My first trip to Kansas proved to be quite an adventure! And there were lots of twists and turns along the way. For years, I had this dream: to participate in the annual international autoharp contest at the Walnut Valley Bluegrass Festival, held every September in Winfield, Kansas. I heard about it through *The Autoharpaholic*. I had even met one of the festival's first place autoharp contest winners who had recently moved to the Twin Cities to teach music there.

In the fall of 2003, I finally got the chance to go, thanks to some friends I knew from church, a couple about my age and their daughter. Harlan and Kay had been attending the festival for years, while their daughter Marcia came occasionally. They offered me a ride there and back. But since I couldn't afford to stay at a motel like them, I brought along my tent and decided to stay at a campsite adjoining the festival grounds. I also brought along a chromaharp (an instrument similar to an autoharp) which I had bought on sale for $50 at a Minneapolis music store, and had recently converted to diatonic tuning.

The ride to Kansas was uneventful until the tail end. After starting out from the Twin Cities around 8 in the morning, we arrived in Winfield twelve hours later around 7:30 pm, just before it got dark. However, before reaching the city outskirts, we ran into a huge thunderstorm. The wind howled, the lightning flashed, and the thunder roared. The rain came down in sheets, making driving almost impossible. We could barely see the road ahead. Harlan, who was driving, assured me that the weather hadn't ever been this bad during their previous visits. In fact, they were expecting temperatures in the nineties.

Fortunately, we got to the festival grounds safely. But when we arrived, we ran into another glitch. The festival ticket taker wouldn't allow Kay and Harlan to drive me to the campsite because they didn't have a ticket for that day. So, they drove me to a border fence surrounding the campsite where they threw my gear over it. It was an illegal procedure, but fortunately we weren't caught. The next day, Kay gave the ticket taker a piece of her mind, but it made no difference. He wouldn't budge from his rigid stance. To him, rules were rules, and there were no exceptions, rain or shine.

By the time I finally made it to the campsite to pitch my tent, the storm that had hit us earlier on the outskirts of Winfield, now arrived full blast at the campsite itself. It poured as I tried in vain to pitch my tent. Fortunately, I had the presence of mind to ask a neighboring camper to help me out. He was nice enough to let me take shelter in his camper until the rain subsided a little. After he stored the rest of my gear under a tarp near his camper, he helped me put up my tent so it wouldn't get wet. However, as soon as my tent was up, the rain started pouring again. I got soaking wet. I quickly took shelter in his camper so I could get warm. He and his wife then turned on the radio to get weather updates. They were predicting thunderstorms until midnight.

By the time I finally got back into my tent, my clothes were soaking wet, as well as the bottom of my sleeping bag. I tried in vain to sleep in my wet T-shirt, but I was so miserable, I had to take it off. Then I tried staying as warm as I could by burrowing into the top dry portion of my sleeping bag, but it was no use. To make matters worse, because of my recent prostate problems, I had to get up around six times at night to relieve myself at a nearby Porto-Potty. In the meantime, it continued to rain all night. Fortunately, my tent withstood the deluge. But by the time I finally got up around eight the next morning, I'd only gotten about two hours of sleep.

II

Of course, the next day was the day of the international autoharp contest which I'd been looking forward to for so long. It was to take place at 10 that morning. At least, the weather turned nice so that I was able to dry out my tent. After the sun came up, the sky turned blue, and it started to warm up. I hurried on over to the campsite bathroom to take a quick shower before getting dressed to go to the festival grounds. But here I ran into another problem. Showers not only cost $3.00, but the shower head was about two feet above my head, so I had to pull on a chord with one hand while washing myself with the other. At least the water was nice and warm.

When I finally got to the festival grounds, I had about half an hour to spare before the contest started. In the meantime, Harlan, Kay, and Marcia showed up in their van with my autoharp in tow, and wished me good luck. They stayed for the entire contest so they could hear me play. They also took lots of pictures. I rushed to an area next to the barn where the contest was to take place in order to tune my harp. There I ran into some of the other contestants who were also tuning their autoharps. I was in awe of the beautiful harps I saw. Some were built by nationally acclaimed luthiers like George Orthey. I talked to several other contestants most of whom were quite friendly, albeit nervous like me. One was a lady named Anne who ended up winning first place.

Then at last, my big moment arrived! The emcee summoned all of us back stage where he read out the contest rules. Each contestant was given a number. My number was seven, the date of my birth. There were thirteen contestants from ten different states. Each one was asked to play two instrumental pieces. They were not to say anything by way of introduction. The judges' decisions were based solely on what they heard. They weren't given the names of the contestants. Five finalists were picked from those competing. They were allowed to play two more instrumentals for the second round. And from that round, three winners were chosen. Each winner received a brand-new luthier-made harp. One of the rules stipulated that no medleys were allowed. This affected me since I had prepared a medley of Bach's *Jesu of Man's Desiring* along with Beethoven's *Ode to Joy*. Therefore, I had to make a last-minute adjustment.

After the contest rules were read to the contestants, I went to the back of the barn to where Kay, Harlan, and Marcia were sitting. As I listened to the first few contestants, I was awestruck by the high quality of their performances. I had never heard anyone play that well except my teacher Stevie, Karen Mueller, and Bryan Bowers. When the emcee called out contestant number five, I walked to the back of the barn behind the stage to await my turn. By now the adrenaline was really flowing! Yes, the moment I had dreamed about all these years had finally arrived!

Before I could give it any more thought, the emcee called out my number. I proceeded to walk slowly to the front of the stage where I took a seat. I knew there was an audience out there, but I was much too nervous to make any eye contact. I proceeded to launch into my first piece, Bach's J*esu, Joy of Man's Desiring*. While playing it, I knew right away that this wasn't the best performance I was capable of. I was much too nervous. My hands were shaking as I rushed through the piece. I also realized too late that my harp was slightly out of tune. I now remembered that the emcee had mentioned that 40% of the judges' scores were based on the autoharp being in tune.

My second piece, *The Blue Skirt Waltz*, started out much better. I gave it all I had as I played my heart out on one of my favorite tunes. This time I didn't worry about making mistakes or even being out of tune. But now there was another glitch. As I was playing, one of my metal finger picks flew out of my hand onto the stage. "Oh no!" I thought to myself. Yet I managed to finish the piece with no further mishaps. Then, as quickly as it had begun, it was all over! I stumbled off the stage with a profound sense of relief that I had managed to get through my selections.

Now I returned to sit in back of the hall with my friends, so I could hear the rest of the contestants. I was impressed by the fine quality of their performances, as well as the beautiful craftsmanship of their harps. I must admit I felt a twinge of disappointment when my number wasn't called as one of the five finalists. But I wasn't surprised either. I stayed to hear the third, second, and first place winners play their final numbers and receive their prize autoharps. The first-place winner was the woman I had talked with before the contest. She told the audience that this was her first time in Winfield, and that some of her friends had encouraged her to enter the contest. She added that she was so nervous that she didn't know what to say. But her playing more than made up for it. I recalled that one of her pieces was a complex number that contained diminished chords.

After the contest was finished, an elderly lady came up to me to say, "I really loved that piece you played –*The Blue Skirt Waltz*. It's one of my all-time favorites!" Her unexpected compliment almost made up for my disappointment in not winning anything.

III

The rest of the weekend turned out fine. For one thing, the weather continued to be sunny and warm. Friday morning, Kay drove me to a nearby laundromat so I could wash and dry my clothes and sleeping bag. It felt so good to sleep in a dry sleeping bag again for the rest of the festival. Marcia gave me some helpful tips on which performers to check out. So, for the rest of that weekend, I rushed about from stage to stage to catch as many acts as I could. I was also impressed by some of the other contests I attended, especially the fiddle and finger picking guitar contests. I heard some fine bluegrass and old-timey bands that really got my musical juices flowing. While listening to some of the contestants, I thought to myself that it would take me several lifetimes to achieve their level of virtuosity. I took tons of photos.

Although I enjoyed listening to all the fine music, the festival highlight didn't come until Friday night. And it was completely unexpected. As I was walking through the grandstand to check out the instruments, books, tapes, and CDs for sale, I ran into a guy who noticed my harp. He was very eager to have a look at it. So, I got it out of my case. I was a bit embarrassed at first because my instrument wasn't even an autoharp, but a chromaharp. But the man insisted on trying it out. Impressed with its tonal quality, he played several autoharp standards like *Wildwood Flower*. After he finished, I got brave enough to try out some of my own tunes. Afterwards, he gave me his business card and told me he was an instrument buyer for a music store in Texas. Then he showed me one of his autoharps which cost over $1800. I was impressed!

But the evening wasn't over yet. Next, I stopped at a table where I met a woman named Mary Ann who was the editor of the *Autoharp Quarterly*. She sat there next to her husband. Mary Ann recommended various autoharp books, tapes, CDs, and other accessories. She also gave me a complimentary, current copy of *Autoharp Quarterly*. She told me about an autoharp website called

Cyberpluckers that autoharp players from all over the country consulted to share information. But then came the clincher! She told me that my contest performance reminded her of a man named Marty Schumann who had been the first-place champion in the very first international Winfield autoharp contest in 1981. She added that he had only made one CD before his untimely death called Autoharpistry. I purchased a copy immediately, and it quickly became my all-time favorite autoharp recording!

VI

*Well, I had this funny dream the other night,
I saw Bob Dylan in the pale moonlight,
He wore no clothes, his face was a wreck,
He had this harmonica 'round his neck.
When I asked him why he was out so late,
He said it was just a twist of fate:
"On my way to my patron saint,
I got run over by a truck of paint—
Red, white, and blue paint."*

*"So, that explains the tread marks on your chin!"
"That don't mean nothin!" He said with a grin.
Well, now I didn't know what to think,
So, I invited him into this bar for a drink.
But he said he didn't drink no more,
He'd given up booze at the age of four,
Now, all he did was sit around and smoke,
Sit around the house telling Eskimo jokes.
"Have you heard the one about the Eskimo and the ice pick?"
I said: "No, is that one they tell up in Hibbing?'*

*Well, I steered him into this veggie place,
Where I ordered us some suzettes with crape,
I asked him how he'd come so far,
And what it felt like to be a big star.*

"Big star, nothin!" He just grinned into his cup,
And sang this five-hour song he made up
About a nuclear holocaust in which everyone died,
'Xcept him and this cat named Cyanide.
"We were twins, don't you see, both born in May,
And that's why we decided to stay."
When I told him I didn't understand,
He said, "That's O.K. and shook my hand.

Just about then the word got around
That old Bobby Dylan was back in town.
The reporters streamed in with their cameras and notes,
The whole place was buzzin' with flashbulbs and quotes.
But when I looked back to where Dylan had sat,
He disappeared in about two seconds flat.
The whole place turned as empty as a hole in the wall,
With nothing to show that he'd been there at all.

I scratched my head, I thought I'd gone mad,
Or else this was the weirdest dream I ever had,
When this nasal voice said in my ear:
"You're not so bad, but you are pretty queer.
You shoulda seen this joint last year this time,
They was dancin' on tables drinkin' turpentine.
This gal was waltzin' in back with a bear,
With the plates and saucers flyin' everywhere!"

Then old Bobby came back with a smile,
Said, "Gotta go now, but I'll be back in a while,
Just check out that moon when it's pale and thin,
And don't forget about us Cyanide twins!"
Well, I had this funny dream the other night,
I saw Bob Dylan in the pale moonlight,
He wore no clothes, his face was a wreck,
He had a wand in one hand, in the other he had a deck.

My Dylan obsession began in the spring of 1975 while I was living in Namche International House near the U of M campus. I had just dropped out of the English as a Second Language graduate studies, and had completely given up my dreams of teaching abroad. Instead, I felt like I was floundering with no idea of what to do with my life. All this time I was working as a pizza-short order cook at Valli Restaurant in Dinkytown, earning minimum wage and feeling very depressed.

The one thing that saved me from giving up on life was my music. Every chance I got, I played my guitar and harmonica in the basement of Namche House so I wouldn't disturb anybody. I also listened to all the folk-rock records I could get my hands on. Around this time, a friend handed me a small paperback by an author named Anthony Scaduto entitled *Dylan, an Intimate Biography*.

I devoured that book in one sitting like a thirsting man who had just found an oasis in the desert, or a starving man who had just been offered a crust of bread. This book spoke to me like no other reading I had ever done. The only time I had felt this excited was on that Thanksgiving weekend in 1966 when I discovered the world of rock-n-roll music on Gene's transistor radio in Marion Hall.

Scaduto's biography mentioned that Dylan was born in Duluth, grew up in Hibbing, and studied briefly at the U of M. He got started playing folk music at a Dinkytown coffeehouse called the

Ten O'Clock Scholar which used to be located just a few doors down from the Valli restaurant where I worked. Scaduto wrote that Dylan had gotten hooked on the folk songs of Woody Guthrie after reading Woody's own autobiography *Bound for Glory*. In fact, Dylan got so enamored with Woody that he not only learned all his songs, but also assumed Woody's persona and accent during his coffeehouse gigs. Eventually, he got a chance to visit his idol in a New York hospital where Woody was dying of Huntington's Chorea. Reading Scaduto's book made me feel like I wanted to embark on a similar journey.

I dug up all the information about Dylan I could get my hands on. It so happened that another Namche House resident named Lynn was also a big Dylan fan. She clued me in on two Dylan records that would change my life forever: *Another Side of Dylan* and *Blood on the Tracks*. While listening to the opening cut on *Blood on the Tracks, Tangled Up in Blue*, I felt as if I had swallowed lightning. As I listened to both albums over and over again, I felt a torrent of emotions. After that, I started playing all the Dylan songs I could get my hands on. This proved to be difficult because I wasn't able to find that many Dylan songbooks, and it was often hard to figure out the lyrics from listening to his records. But playing those songs helped me relieve all the anguish and frustration I was feeling at the time. That summer, shortly before quitting my dead-end Valli restaurant job, I remember hearing one of Dylan's new songs from Blood on the Tracks on the radio someone had brought into the restaurant. It was called *Lily and the Jack of Hearts*. This song with its driving rhythm, piercing harmonica solo, and riveting lyrics electrified me. I knew right then and there that I wanted a better life for myself than to continue slaving away making pizzas for minimum wage.

II

About three years later, in the fall of 1978, I was working full-time as a mail clerk at the new Hennepin County Medical Center in downtown Minneapolis, when I heard an announcement that Dylan was scheduled to do a live concert at the St. Paul Civic Center on Halloween Night. I could hardly wait to get a ticket since they were going on sale on a first-come-first-served basis at Dayton's Department store downtown. The only problem was that I was scheduled to work that day at HCMC. I also knew that if I waited too long, they would be sold out. Therefore, I made the decision to defy my supervisor, whom I didn't like to begin with, in order to buy a ticket. I waited all day at Dayton's where there was a long line of other hopefuls. But unfortunately, by the time I got to the ticket counter, they were all sold out! My heart sank! Not only that, but by the time I returned to work the next day, my supervisor raked me over the coals for missing an entire workday without telling her. To punish me, she suspended me for three days without pay.

But I wouldn't be denied! I was determined to get a ticket to that concert come what may! To my delight, I saw in the Star Tribune that a scalper was offering to sell tickets for $25 a shot. I called the number listed and got my ticket after all. At this point, I didn't care how much it cost. I was bound and determined to attend that concert! But I wasn't out of the woods yet. On the day of the big event, I came down with a bad cold. Yet I wasn't going to miss this event of a lifetime! I took plenty of cold meds, bundled up tightly, and made it to the Civic Center with plenty of time to spare.

The concert itself turned out to be unforgettable! The center was packed with Dylan fans whom security had to keep from mobbing the raised stage. Dylan bounded onto the stage wearing a hat with a broad brim and feather sticking from it. He was wearing white face like a mime. Backed by his rock band and a trio of women singers, he launched right into his first set. He played all his biggest hits such as *Mr. Tambourine Man, Tangled Up in Blue, Highway 61 Revisited,* and *Like a Rolling Stone.* The enthusiastic audience cheered him on wildly. However, I noticed that Dylan had altered a lot of his song arrangements, so that I often had a hard time recognizing them since they didn't sound at all like his records. But that didn't matter to his adoring fans who hung on every word. They loved every minute. There were lots of encores. His fans didn't want him to leave. At the end of the concert, I saw something I had never seen before, as hundreds of people in the auditorium below stood up and held up cigarette lighters and candles in a vast sea of lights.

There was an important footnote to this concert experience. During the three days of my suspension, I was able to find a better job as an activities aide in a nursing home. It was there that I was able to use my music for the first time as part of my work by leading sing-a-longs and other musical activities.

III

Fifteen years after that memorable concert at the Civic Center, I had another life-changing Dylan experience. It took place in April 1993, a few weeks before Dylan's 52nd birthday. I heard that they were doing a Dylan soundalike contest at the 400 Bar in the Cedar Riverside part of Minneapolis. On a dare, I decided to enter. I signed up with more than forty other contestants, all of whom were vying to sound more like Dylan than Bob himself. The age of the contestants ranged from twelve years to my age or older. Each one was designated with an honorary Dylan after his name. Thus, I became Tony Wentersdorf Dylan. The place was packed!

The participants sang everything from *Sad-eyed Lady of the Low Lands* to *Subterranean Homesick Blues*. Many of the contestants accompanied themselves on the harmonica. A few sang acapella. Three people were selected to judge the contest on criteria like stage presence and sounding most like Dylan. People in the audience were pretty raucous as they got into the act. They let the performers know what they thought of them by holding up signs with numbers from one to ten. Ten meant they really liked the performer, one meant they thought he was lousy. They also heckled the ones they disliked mercilessly, while whooping and hollering their approval for those they favored. It was pure pandemonium!

And as if the whole atmosphere wasn't nerve-wracking enough, there was the added pressure that the whole thing was being televised by a St. Paul public TV station. By the time I was ready to perform, I was sweating bullets! My hands and fingers were shaking as I climbed onto the stage. Then, before I could think about it too much, I launched into my song. It was a song that I had written called *Dylan Talking Dream*. As I poured my heart out, I sensed the audience was right there with me. I heard lots of cheering, especially during my harmonica solos. It seemed to me that the audience was really digging my performance. After I had finished, I got a standing ovation! It was an experience beyond my wildest dreams! Then, as I sat down to listen to the rest of the contestants, I noticed that I was the only one who had sung an original song. All the others did Dylan songs. While sitting there, I fantasized about maybe coming in third place at the most. After an agonizing delay during which the judges made their decisions, the emcee finally read out the results. "Third place: John Eric Thiede Dylan, winner of a Bob Dylan T-shirt; second place: Dan Prozinsky Dylan, winner of a $75 bar tab at the 400 Bar; and first place *(yes, first place; I held my breath!)*, winner of a $200 gift certificate at Northern Lights Music…*(yes, first place!)* Tony Wentersdorf Dylan!"

I couldn't believe my luck as I sat there stunned! Then the emcee motioned me to come back on stage to receive my check. He also asked me to do another song, so I sang one of the few Dylan songs I knew by heart. After that contest, I was floating on a cloud all the way home. It took me a long time to come back to earth.

This story also has an important footnote. I found out later that KTCA-TV not only filmed the entire contest, but also included it as part of a unique show about Minnesota curiosities called *Only in Minnesota*. This show, hosted by Twin Cities comedian Louie Anderson, featured such Minnesota oddities as the annual eel pout festival in Mille Lacs, the polka mass in Duluth, the world's largest ball of twine in Darwin, the Kensington rune stone, and, of course, the annual Dylan soundalike contest. I got my fifteen seconds worth of fame as they showed a short clip of the contest in future broadcasts. The only downside was that they misspelled my last name as Wintersdorf. But that was just a small wrinkle in the biggest thrill of my life! And I owe it all to Bob!

AFTERWORD

Yes, I have indeed been blessed by many things in my life. Although I've suffered from major depression and anxiety for most of my adulthood, I've also gotten a lot of help along the way. There have been wonderful therapists, day-treatment programs, therapy groups, support groups, Dialectical Behavior Therapy (DBT) classes, Adult Rehabilitative Mental Health Services workers, the National Alliance on Mental Illness, and, of course, that residential treatment center that had such a tremendous impact on my life. I have all these to thank. Of course, I've also had some bad experiences with a few therapists and therapy programs such as one abusive day-treatment program I attended some 35 years ago. But, on the whole, my experiences have been very positive, and I've got a lot to be grateful for. I've also gotten a lot of support from my church community and friends who have stood by me through good times and bad.

The other thing I'm very grateful for are my creative gifts, especially music. Yes, my love of music has sustained me throughout my life, giving it meaning and purpose. Music has provided me with an important means of connnecting with others. In fact, I've gotten to know many of my closest friends through music. And many of my peak life experiences relate to music. From the time I was a three-year old pre-schooler in Germany who came home singing a German kids' song, to my discovery of the autoharp in 1976, and my winning the Bob Dylan soundalike contest in 1993, music has always had a profound impact on my life.